Haggard
An Entertainment

Eric Chappell

Based on characters created
by Michael Green

A SAMUEL FRENCH ACTING EDITION

SAMUEL FRENCH

FOUNDED 1830

SAMUELFRENCH.COM
SAMUELFRENCH-LONDON.CO.UK

MUSIC USE NOTE

CHARACTERS

LANDLORD

HAGGARD

GRUNGE

BETTY BOUNCER

RODERICK

GENT

FANNY FOULACRE

SIR JOSH FOULACRE

LADY TARTLET

ONE-EYED WILL

THE HOOK

LORD CHESTERFIELD

LORD TARTLET

VICAR

NELLY BLIGHT

SEAMAN

PREACHER

DEATH

CATESBY

TIBBS

ELUSIVE EDWARD

SETTING

Composite set representing in turn a country inn, Lady Tartlet's
withdrawing room, Haggard Hall and a prison cell.

TIME

Regency Period

AUTHOR'S NOTE

Haggard is something of an undisciplined romp. Scenes may be cut,
music and songs added and actors may take several parts. It is important
that they have a good time short of chewing up the scenery.

INTRODUCTION

When I came to adapt *Squire Haggard's Diary* for television I found I needed an accomplice to assist Haggard in his scheming, so I introduced a new leading character, Nathaniel Grunge. Grunge was a menial who resented his lowly position, had a gift for prophecy, and was as crafty as his master. He was played by the superb Sam Kelly.

For the role of Roderick I asked for Reece Dinsdale, so good in *Home to Roost*. Reece made the part more romantic, less dithering, but still concerned for his personal safety.

Keith Baron, another old mate, from *Duty Free*, played the immortal Haggard. Keith found Haggard, brilliantly conceived by Michael Green, a gift to play, as I did to write.

Years later when I decided to put the series on the stage I tried it out in two productions. The first was enjoyed by the audience but I felt it lacked something. I decided it was anarchy.

In the second production I allowed my three characters, already straining at the leash, to go mad. The effect was contagious. People burst into song, women vied to play the men's parts, anachronisms abounded, and everyone went Regency. The result was a glorious romp and a good time was had by all – including the audience.

– Eric Chappell

THE STORY OF SQUIRE HAGGARD

Squire Haggard was born in a damp cellar under Northampton Market Square in 1943 when I was a cub reporter on the Northampton evening paper, *The Chronicle and Echo*. They also published a weekly paper, the *Northampton Mercury*, which had the distinction of being one of the oldest newspapers in the world, with files going back to1729. Each week the paper printed an extract from the files of 200 years previously. Compiling this item was usually given to me (along with making the tea) and I spent hours in the basement turning over the files. At first, it was just a chore but then I began to get fascinated by the glimpses of eighteenth century life disclosed. Eventually, the Chief Reporter had to send someone down to fetch me up.

Reports of hangings were frequent, often for what would today be considered a minor crime, such as stealing a pig. One man was hanged for stealing two shillings. But surely the most unfortunate case was that of one John Wild, who was sentenced to be transported to the colonies and then later to death for "returning before his time". Presumably he hitched a lift.

Illness featured heavily, with lists of mortalities. Few diseases had their modern name. Some had picturesque titles such as Stoppage of the Blood or Griping of the Guts. Others were blamed on foreigners, such as The French Disease (syphilis) or The Spanish Fever. Then there were The Blains, The Boils and The Windy Spasms. Not to mention Worms, Scurvy, Wind, The Stone and Gravel. One woman with dropsy was tapped 48 times to remove the fluid and yielded 12 barrels, 12 gallons and two pints.

Much of this interesting information had been brought to town in the 1700s by a courier with two pistols stuffed in his boots who would gallop into the Market Square where the editor was waiting to greet him. I could look out of the office window and see the same market square, little changed.

Soon afterwards I joined millions of other young men in the wartime army. Boredom is the curse of the soldier and I read avidly anything that came to hand. I was already fascinated by the eighteenth century from my experiences in the basement. Then I found Boswell's *Life of Johnson* in the camp library and became hooked on 18th century diaries. The drinking habits of the diarists left me gasping. Even Dr. Johnson could drink three bottles of claret at dinner. And their hypocrisy was outrageous. Boswell complained he was too ill to go to church while suffering from venereal disease brought on by his own drunken fornication. Naturally, he blamed the woman for infecting him. Another diarist was Parson Woodford, who drank a bottle of port every day for starters. He had strange dishes on the table – "Pigge's face"; rook pie; "Branes";

Pease pudding; and "a lung with roots". He was quite partial to a dish of larks as well. And afterwards, a "plumb pudding".

Woodford, along with others such as Pepys a century before him, had an obsession with small sums of money and would dutifully record, "lost 0.0.2d at cribbage". Not surprising, if he'd had his usual ration of port.

Demobbed, I returned to Northampton and started an occasional column satirising those old diaries. It was supposed to be the diary of a 1777 squire, whose idea of fun was getting drunk and evicting a crippled old lady. I forget the squire's name, but it wasn't Haggard in those days. He vanished when I went to London but reappeared a few years later when the *Daily Telegraph* asked me to contribute to their new satirical column Peter Simple, brilliantly compiled by Michael Wharton, who suggested the name Haggard.

A typical entry might go something like this:

Dec 25: Rain. Jas. Kneebone d. From the Howling Spasms. This day being that most sacred feast in the calendar, viz. Quarter Day, I sallied forth in a.m. to evict those behind with their rent. The first was old Granny Hayseed who snivelled, "Do you not know which day it is?" to which I replied, "Yes, Rent Day" which caused me so much mirth I fell in a Spasm.

Shot an interesting trespasser in p.m. After he fled I remembered it might have been my brother- in- law who sometimes walks over on Christmas Day.

Dec 26: Hail. Jeremiah Barnwood dead from the Black Eruption. My servant Grunge came to return the old pair of breeches I gave him for Christmas. He said there was a huge hole in them. This I knew full well, since it had been bitten out by Lady Constance Bedwell in a fit of passion after the Hunt Ball last year. Gave him a piece of coal instead and he left crying "God bless you for a fine old English gentleman, sir".

The Squire had his TV debut in a BBC programme called Grubstreet, about the humorous columns of Fleet Street. In 1975 I turned his adventures into a book and in 1990 Eric Chappell of *Rising Damp* fame transformed it into two hilarious TV series for Yorkshire TV, starring Keith Baron as the Squire and Sam Kelly as Grunge, after which *The Telegraph* promoted the squire to his own column.

Now Eric Chappell has brought new life to the outrageous old devil with a stage version which takes the squire away from his pen and his diary and out into the wider world and lets us see his boozing, conniving and lusting for real. Enough to make even a sufferer from Rising of the Tripes laugh.

– Michael Green

For Keith Barron, Reece Dinsdale and Sam Kelly

ACT ONE

Scene One – Gingerbread

(The set is a composite one representing in turn a country inn, Haggard Hall, Lady Tartlet's withdrawing room and, finally, a prison cell. There are long tables, benches, pillars, a fireplace, and a high window.)

(Int. of The Swan With Two Necks. A few nights before Christmas.)

(Solitary drinkers sit around the corners of the room.)

(HAGGARD enters with a flourish and takes a seat by the fire. He is a mean looking man in a shabby coat and soiled lace. A surly LANDLORD advances to meet him.)

LANDLORD. Sir?

HAGGARD. Bring me a brace of pheasants, well hung. A plump capon. A side of beef – if tender. Potatoes roasted and two bottles of your best Madeira.

LANDLORD. *(dryly)* Will that be all?

HAGGARD. Yes. I dine alone.

LANDLORD. Not here you don't.

HAGGARD. What! You refuse to serve me, you dog?

LANDLORD. I do.

HAGGARD. Then take care. You are obliged to provide comfort and sustenance to the weary traveller. That is the law.

LANDLORD. Are you a traveller?

HAGGARD. I am.

LANDLORD. Then keep going.

HAGGARD. Be warned. I am a magistrate.

LANDLORD. I know you're a magistrate, Haggard. But judge not lest you be judged – for on the great day all will be judged and all will be equal.

HAGGARD. What!

LANDLORD. And don't ask for credit because refusal often offends…

(The **LANDLORD** *exits with a sneer.* **GRUNGE**, *a menial, enters. He is about the same age as* **HAGGARD** *and equally down at heel. He hovers uncertainly.)*

HAGGARD. What is it, Grunge?

GRUNGE. I thought I might warm myself by the fire, sir.

HAGGARD. Well, don't stand too close or the dog will charge you for it.

GRUNGE. Has he refused you credit?

HAGGARD. Not only that – he presumed to speak to me as an equal.

GRUNGE. They say in France that all men are born equal.

HAGGARD. You weren't, Grunge, you were born under a hedge.

GRUNGE. They talk of liberty, equality and fraternity. They say one day the rivers will run red with the blood of the aristocracy.

HAGGARD. *(frowns)* Have you been talking to the landlord?

GRUNGE. No, sir?

HAGGARD. Then take note. I'm not interested in what a nation of onion nibblers and mincing dressmakers has to say – and if you repeat these lies I'll have you whipped from here to Haggard Hall.

GRUNGE. Yes, sir.

*(***GRUNGE** *moves downstage.)*

(bitter aside) They'll pay one day. Those that stretch themselves on beds of down – those that grind our faces and flay our skins. What are their rustling silks and velvets but the sweat of our brows and the wants of our bellies.

HAGGARD. What was that, Grunge?

(**GRUNGE** *turns innocently.*)

GRUNGE. I was merely observing that times are changing. *(becomes mystical)* I see a time when there will be no more hardship. When the forces of nature will serve the poorest of men. When the electric fluid will drive mighty engines, illuminate our streets, turning night into day. I see a time when our homes will be warmed and water heated by this same power and there'll be baths for everyone.

HAGGARD. Well, that won't suit you, you verminous rogue.

(**BETTY**, *a buxom serving wench enters and begins cleaning the tables.*)

(**HAGGARD** *watches her with evident approval as she crosses the room.*)

HAGGARD. By thunder, Grunge. I haven't seen jellies like that since the Lord Mayor's banquet. Who is she?

GRUNGE. That's Betty. Betty Bouncer – the new serving wench. You knew her sister.

HAGGARD. Of course – the Bouncers – I knew them well.

(**BETTY** *approaches and gives* **HAGGARD** *a hostile glance.*)

GRUNGE. What news, Betty?

BETTY. *(glumly)* The plague's raging in Vienna and James Soper has been hanged for stealing a nail. His last words were 'may you all rot'.

HAGGARD. I'm sure he didn't mean me, Betty. I'm a sad figure – all alone in that empty house...

BETTY. What of your wife?

HAGGARD. Gone to Bath to take the waters – so I'm all alone...in that big empty house...

BETTY. Are you indeed?

(*She crosses to serve a customer.*)

HAGGARD. *(sighs)* See how they treat me, Grunge. There was a time when my credit would have been good until harvest. Now my debts stretch out before me like a whore in bed – and it's a long time since I've seen one of those. *(pause)* We'll have to evict someone.

GRUNGE. So near Christmas?

HAGGARD. Why not? We'll evict Granny Acorn.

GRUNGE. They say she's a witch.

HAGGARD. Superstitious nonsense.

GRUNGE. Amos Bindweed said it was nonsense – now he's a stoat.

HAGGARD. He's not a stoat.

GRUNGE. They found a stoat sitting in his chair.

HAGGARD. I don't care if they found a stoat sitting in his chair, wearing his slippers and taking snuff. Amos Bindweed planted that stoat to fool his creditors – and I'll have to do the same if things don't improve. *(sighs)* I haven't even the price of a bottle of Madeira.

GRUNGE. I have a shilling.

HAGGARD. A shilling! How came you by it?

GRUNGE. I sold my body on death to the anatomists.

HAGGARD. You sold your body for a shilling?

GRUNGE. Yes, sir.

HAGGARD. You got a bargain, Grunge.

(He takes the shilling from him.)

You may join me.

(GRUNGE sits.)

(HAGGARD catches BETTY's arm as she passes.)

HAGGARD. How's your sister, Betty?

BETTY. She's a great sorrow to us. She was debauched by a gentleman and ran away to London.

HAGGARD. How sad.

(He turns the coin over in his hands.)

Know what this is, Betty? A silver shilling.

BETTY. A silver shilling. I haven't seen one of those since my sister left home.

HAGGARD. It could be yours – and more. This is nothing. I can give you a greater gift. I can make you a lady of quality.

BETTY. How so?

HAGGARD. Come to the Hall tonight and I shall dress you in silks and satins.

BETTY. That's what you told my sister. Now she's selling gingerbread on London Bridge.

*(**HAGGARD** leers at **GRUNGE**.)*

HAGGARD. Gingerbread… *(another leer)* And do you have a little gingerbread for me, Betty?

BETTY. Certainly not. You wouldn't cover me in silks and satins – not while you've got a hole in your britches.

(She flounces off.)

*(**HAGGARD** sighs and calls to the passing **LANDLORD**.)*

HAGGARD. Landlord, a bottle of your best Madeira.

(He gives him a coin.)

*(The **LANDLORD** examines the coin carefully then bites it thoughtfully before exiting.)*

Did you see that? I thought the cur was going to eat it.

*(**RODERICK HAGGARD** enters from the yard. He is a younger version of his father but dressed with more care.)*

Roderick! What are you doing here?

RODERICK. I've been sent down, father.

HAGGARD. Why?

RODERICK. I threw a chamber pot at the dean.

HAGGARD. I've told you before – that's not funny, Roderick.

RODERICK. It wasn't meant to be. He wanted settlement of my college debts.

HAGGARD. *(sighs)* I cannot pay them, Roderick. We're staring ruin in the face.

RODERICK. Never mind, father. I shall soon be as rich as a London alderman. I'm almost engaged to a lady of quality with ten thousand in the funds.

HAGGARD. What!

RODERICK. She's the only daughter of Sir Josh Foulacre and when he dies she inherits the whole estate.

HAGGARD. Then let's drink to his early death. Landlord, another glass. *(pause)* One moment, you said <u>almost</u> engaged.

RODERICK. Her father doesn't like me.

GRUNGE. *(quietly)* That's a surprise.

HAGGARD. Why not?

RODERICK. He hates fortune hunters above all men.

GRUNGE. He's fought three duels to defend her honour.

RODERICK. And that is why I must meet Fanny in secret. She arrives today on the London stage.

HAGGARD. Then book a room. You must make Fanny yours within the hour.

RODERICK. But I have no money. I spent my last crown on gingerbread.

HAGGARD. *(grins)* You young dog. Nevertheless you shall have money. Hurry.

(**RODERICK** *exits into hall.*)

HAGGARD. We need money, Grunge.

GRUNGE. Money…

(*He looks around. He takes a ring from his finger.*)

Then what about the ring and the rustic…?

HAGGARD. The ring and the rustic…? Do you think it'll work?

GRUNGE. It's worked before…

HAGGARD. Then let's give it a whirl…

(**GRUNGE** *winks and exits.*)

(**HAGGARD** *looks about the room. He selects a solitary drinker, a superior young man. He approaches and begins peering about the floor.*)

GENT. *(curiously)* Have you lost something, sir?

HAGGARD. Yes. I mislaid a ring in here last night. It is of no great worth but of considerable sentimental value.

GENT. *(looking)* Would you describe it?

HAGGARD. It was a simple gold ring with a green stone. It was given to me by His Royal Highness the Prince of Wales.

GENT. *(impressed)* The Prince!

HAGGARD. We caroused together when we were young and when I returned to the shires he gave me the ring to remember him by. I would not be parted from it for all my wealth. I intend to post a reward of a hundred guineas for its safe return.

GENT. A hundred guineas!

HAGGARD. I must see the landlord...

(*He exits stage left being careful to cover the hole in his britches.*)

(*The young gentleman begins to look about.* **GRUNGE** *enters stage right. There is straw in his hair and he's chewing on a blade of grass. He is singing softly to himself.*)

GRUNGE. *(mummerset)* 'Oi've just come up rom Zummerset where the coider apples grow...etc.'

GENT. Get out of here, fellow – this room is for gentlemen.

GRUNGE. I know that, sir. But I seek the advice of a gentleman. I found this ring in the dust outside and wondered if it was of any value...

GENT. Let me see...

(*He examines the ring.*)

GENT. It has no value. The stone is glass and the gold is pinchbeck.

GRUNGE. *(sighs)* I thought not.

GENT. But stay – it takes my fancy. I'll give you a guinea for it.

GRUNGE. Ah, but it takes my fancy, too.

GENT. Then should we say five?

GRUNGE. It still takes my fancy…

GENT. Then ten and be damned to you. What do you say?

GRUNGE. Oi may be cabbage looking but I aint green. Oi think you want it enough to pay thirty…

GENT. *(hesitates)* Then thirty it is and the devil take you.

(**GRUNGE** *takes the money.*)

GRUNGE. Now I'll be able to buy the meadow I set my heart upon, and a few cows, and marry my childhood sweetheart. But first – some gingerbread.

(**GRUNGE** *exits into yard.*)

(**HAGGARD** *enters from kitchens.*)

GENT. Great news, sir. I have found the ring and claim the reward.

(He hands ring to **HAGGARD**.*)*

HAGGARD. *(angrily)* The ring! The stone is glass – the gold is pinchbeck. Do you think the Prince would give me this piece of tat?

GENT. But I gave thirty guineas for it.

HAGGARD. Then more fool you, sir.

GENT. That conniving bumpkin!

(He exits thoughtfully.)

(**GRUNGE** *enters stage left carrying smock over his arm.*)

(**HAGGARD** *catches his arm.*)

HAGGARD. *(silkily)* How did we do, Grunge?

GRUNGE. Twenty-five.

HAGGARD. Thirty, you rogue.

(He takes the money from him.)

Try that again and I'll cut your ears off and allow that hat to fall over your eyes.

(**RODERICK** *enters.*)

RODERICK. The landlord won't prepare the room until he's paid.

(**HAGGARD** *hands* **RODERICK** *the money.*)

HAGGARD. Then here's payment – and more.

RODERICK. Where did this come from?

HAGGARD. Let's say it's your allowance...that should impress the lady. Make sure she hears the guineas chink.

RODERICK. God bless you, father.

(*He exits stage left.*)

(**GRUNGE** *sees the young gentleman approaching. He drops the smock on a chair, tips his hat over his eyes and sidles out. The young gentleman picks up the smock and glances from* **GRUNGE** *to* **HAGGARD**.)

(**HAGGARD** *looks innocent and crosses to his seat by the fire. The young man exits, again looking thoughtful, and carrying smock.*)

(**FANNY FOULACRE** *enters. She is finely dressed and fluttering her fan in an agitated manner. She has the habit of talking to herself in asides. She moves downstage.* **HAGGARD** *watches her curiously.*)

FANNY. Where is Roderick? He promised to be here. I'm a woman alone – in a tavern. Tongues will wag. I must remain calm. I've grown quite pale.

(*She pinches her cheeks, she continues striding and fluttering.*)

No one must know. I must dissemble...

(**HAGGARD** *approaches.*)

HAGGARD. You must be Fanny. Fanny Foulacre...

(*The fan flies out of* **FANNY**'s *hand.*)

FANNY. I am undone!!

(HAGGARD *retrieves the fan.*)

HAGGARD. My name is Haggard.

(*A horse neighs in panic from the stables.*)

I'm Roderick's father.

(FANNY *moves further down stage.*)

FANNY. Roderick's father. What a grim visage...

HAGGARD. Since you're travelling alone may I offer you my protection?

(*He gestures to a chair.*)

FANNY. (*further downstage*) His protection. But who will protect me from him? Still, I must be condescending...

(HAGGARD *stares over* FANNY's *shoulder to see whom she's addressing. Finds himself staring into space. She smiles sweetly and joins* HAGGARD *at the table.*)

My father will be here within the hour.

HAGGARD. (*leers*) Time enough.

FANNY. Time enough?

HAGGARD. To become acquainted...

FANNY. Acquainted?

HAGGARD. With Roderick.

FANNY. (*busy with fan*) Roderick! Is he here?

HAGGARD. You're sitting in his chair.

FANNY. Oh! It's still warm.

HAGGARD. He's a hot blooded youth.

FANNY. To think we're so close!

HAGGARD. You could become closer still...

FANNY. How so?

HAGGARD. He's having a room prepared...

FANNY. (*shocked*) What! Would he anticipate the lawful rites of matrimony?

HAGGARD. Indeed not, my lady. It's so that you make take some light refreshment – and possibly a little gingerbread...

(RODERICK enters.)

FANNY. Roderick!

RODERICK. Fanny!

(She hurls herself at him and kisses him furiously.)

(HAGGARD looks discreetly away.)

(FANNY breaks away.)

FANNY. We must be circumspect.

RODERICK. Of course.

FANNY. And discrete.

RODERICK. Discretion is my watchword.

(He embraces her. She breaks away and moves downstage.)

FANNY. I am transported.

(She breathes heavily.)

(RODERICK takes her by the hand.)

RODERICK. Let me work a metaphor. Fanny.

(He sits her at a table and takes an orange from the bowl.)

You are this orange.

(She stares at the orange.)

FANNY. Oh.

RODERICK. Bright and dazzling and cool to the touch. But peel back the skin and what is revealed?

(He peels back the skin. The orange looks rather soggy.)

The soft and succulent flesh beneath, sweet to the taste...

(He sucks noisily at the orange. He lowers his voice.)

Yield to me even as this orange does...

(The fan begins to flutter furiously. They become aware of the threatening figure of **SIR JOSH FOULACRE** *standing over them.)*

SIR JOSH. Fanny! What is this? I arrive a few minutes late to find you alone in a tavern with this limb of Satan.

FANNY. Not alone, father. I am chaperoned.

SIR JOSH. Chaperoned?

*(***HAGGARD*** stands.)*

RODERICK. My father, sir.

HAGGARD. Your servant, sir.

(He bows. A faint ripping sound.)

SIR JOSH. You are Haggard?

(A horse neighs in panic off.)

HAGGARD. The same.

SIR JOSH. Then you confirm what I've heard. That you've been broken on the exchange and your estate is mortgaged.

HAGGARD. A malicious rumour. Why do you believe such lies?

SIR JOSH. Because you have a hole in your britches and your jacket is torn.

HAGGARD. I've spent all day in the coverts, sir. I may dress frugally but I'm an indulgent parent. Roderick, show Sir Josh the extent of my generosity.

*(***RODERICK*** smiles and produces the ring.)*

*(***SIR JOSH*** examines the ring.)*

SIR JOSH. This ring is worthless. The stone is glass and the gold is pinchbeck.

HAGGARD. What!

(He stares in horror at the ring.)

RODERICK. That may be so. But it's worth a hundred guineas.

HAGGARD. *(weakly)* A hundred guineas...

SIR JOSH. If you think that ring is worth a hundred guineas, you're a fool, sir. And a knave, if you seek to seduce my daughter with this bauble.

FANNY. He's not a knave, father. All he proposed was that we should pause for a little gingerbread.

SIR JOSH. *(suspiciously)* Gingerbread.

(The **LANDORD** *approaches.)*

LANDLORD. The room is ready for you and the young lady, sir.

SIR JOSH. What! Would you procure my daughter? Stay clear of me, you knaves, or you will taste powder and shot to season your gingerbread.

(He drags **FANNY** *from the room.)*

*(***HAGGARD** *stares in silence at* **RODERICK** *for a moment. He sighs and examines the ring.)*

HAGGARD. A hundred guineas, Roderick?

RODERICK. I met this very nice young man who'd lost this same ring.

HAGGARD. And was it of great sentimental value?

RODERICK. How did you know?

HAGGARD. Just a wild guess. And did this nice young man offer a reward?

RODERICK. He's posting a reward of a hundred guineas. And here's a coincidence.

HAGGARD. I think I can see it coming.

RODERICK. Would you believe it? I met a bumpkin who had found this same ring and didn't know its value. I was able to buy it from him for a fraction of its worth. Now I must find the young man...

HAGGARD. *(sighs)* I don't think you're going to, Roderick. Now tell me gently – did you give all your money for the ring?

RODERICK. Good lord, no. *(winks)* I kept a little back for gingerbread...

(HAGGARD brightens.)

HAGGARD. Gingerbread!

(He regards BETTY lustfully as she bends low over the table.)

RODERICK. I know how much you like it, father.

HAGGARD. I do indeed, Roderick.

(He holds out his palm still regarding BETTY.)

(RODERICK hands him a bag of gingerbread. HAGGARD looks down and groans.)

Scene Two – Daring Deeds

(The Swan With Two Necks. Evening. **HAGGARD**, **RODERICK** *and* **GRUNGE** *enter to find the room deserted. They are greeted by* **BETTY**.*)*

HAGGARD. Quiet tonight, Betty. Is this further evidence of the recession?

BETTY. No sir. We had a visit from One-eyed Will and The Hook last week and the customers are still fearful.

RODERICK. One-eyed Will and The Hook?

HAGGARD. Why do you blanche, Roderick?

RODERICK. They're the notorious tavern brawlers and bullies, father. Have you not seen the posters?

GRUNGE. Aye, the whole town goes in fear of them.

RODERICK. They say that One-eyed Will is terrible but The Hook is worse.

BETTY. Aye, many crimes are laid at their door but none dare inform.

GRUNGE. They abuse women and terrify the populace.

RODERICK. We read of their exploits daily. What were they like, Betty?

BETTY. One-eyed Will is taller and has a hunch.

HAGGARD. *(dryly)* As if one eye isn't enough.

BETTY. The Hook is smaller and has a hook for a hand.

GRUNGE. Aye, smaller but twice as dangerous.

BETTY. He's very sensitive about the hook. If you as much as look at the hook...

RODERICK. What, Betty?

BETTY. There's a brawl.

RODERICK. They won't be coming back, will they, Betty?

BETTY. I should hope not – the Watch have driven them out of the town.

RODERICK. That's a relief.

HAGGARD. You're not afraid, are you, Roderick?

RODERICK. Not for myself but Fanny and her aunt rest here this evening on their way to London.

HAGGARD. Her aunt – Lady Tartlet?

RODERICK. Yes, and she's more fearful than any tavern brawler.

HAGGARD. Well, I hope you get the colour back in your cheeks before they come. Remember, faint heart never won fair lady.

GRUNGE. That gives me an idea – I've been thinking –

HAGGARD. Don't, Grunge – you know it gives you a headache.

GRUNGE. Suppose Master Roderick was to save Fanny from a terrible fate by a deed of daring? Wouldn't her father be forever grateful?

HAGGARD. But that's hardly likely, is it? Look at the way he quaked at the very thought of One-eyed Will and The Hook.

GRUNGE. Ah, but suppose he was to save her from drowning say?

HAGGARD. Drowning?

GRUNGE. That lake of theirs is dark and deep. Suppose she was to fall in...?

RODERICK. Grunge, she's played about that lake since she was a child – she's hardly likely to fall in.

GRUNGE. She would...if she was pushed from the bridge – then you could leap in and save her.

RODERICK. Oh, I see, someone pushes Fanny from the bridge just as I happen to be passing – a large coincidence, Grunge.

(**HAGGARD** *and* **GRUNGE** *exchange glances.*)

HAGGARD. *(sighs)* It wouldn't be a coincidence, Roderick.

RODERICK. I know what would be.

HAGGARD. What?

RODERICK. That I'd learned to swim in the meantime.

GRUNGE. It was just a thought.

HAGGARD. And a good one, Grunge. You've put me in mind of a stratagem. Didn't you say that the ladies travel alone, Roderick?

RODERICK. Yes.

HAGGARD. Good. Women who travel alone are particularly vulnerable. Suppose Grunge and I enter the inn, heavily disguised, and menace the ladies. Then Roderick arrives in the nick of time and puts us to flight?

RODERICK. Heavily disguised?

HAGGARD. As One-eyed Will and The Hook.

RODERICK. But Fanny would recognise you.

HAGGARD. No because no one dare look at One-eyed Will and The Hook. All I'd need is an eye patch and a cushion up my back and Grunge could be The Hook.

GRUNGE. I'm not having my hand off.

HAGGARD. Of course you won't have your hand off. All you'll need is a butcher's hook from the kitchen and your sleeve pulled down.

GRUNGE. It won't work.

HAGGARD. It will. I'll do the difficult bit – all you have to do is glower.

RODERICK. But what do I do?

HAGGARD. Before we start the ravishing you approach, make some slighting remark – seize Grunge by the throat, shake him thus...

*(He begins to shake **GRUNGE** furiously.)*

Hurl him to the ground.

*(**GRUNGE** is hurled to the ground.)*

Stamp on him.

*(He stamps on **GRUNGE**.)*

Then drag his inert body to the door and hurl him down the steps.

*(**GRUNGE** picks himself up indignantly.)*

RODERICK. And what of you, father? What do I do to you?

HAGGARD. Nothing.

(**GRUNGE** *looks more indignant.*)

You quell me with a glance. You point towards the door and I slink away. All bullies are cowards at heart.

GRUNGE. Why can't I slink away?

HAGGARD. We can't both slink away, Grunge. It wouldn't be convincing.

GRUNGE. Why can't I be One-eyed Will?

HAGGARD. You're not tall enough. Don't complain – you have the best part.

GRUNGE. The best part! An inert body! I'm not being an inert body for anyone.

HAGGARD. Grunge, if we succeed in this, Fanny's father will be forever grateful. Our fortunes will be made, yours included. You have a mother, have you not?

GRUNGE. (*hesitates*) There's a woman who claims to be my mother...

HAGGARD. Does she still live in that hollow tree?

GRUNGE. Yes.

HAGGARD. Wouldn't you like to buy her a house with windows and doors? You could if our ruse succeeds.

(*Sounds off.* **HAGGARD** *listens.*)

The ladies have arrived. Come, Grunge – we must prepare ourselves...

(*He drags* **GRUNGE** *out of one door as* **FANNY** *and* **LADY TARTLET** *and the* **LANDLORD** *enter through the other.*)

(**LADY TARTLET** *is a lady in her forties. A severe looking woman in fine clothes.* **RODERICK** *retreats nervously to the far side of the room.*)

(**FANNY** *sees him and becomes flustered. She moves downstage.*)

FANNY. (*aside*) It is he!

LADY T. *(frowns)* What is it, Fanny?

FANNY. Nothing, Aunt.

(Becomes agitated with her fan.)

(aside) Nothing! Only the love of my life.

(LADY TARTLET *eyes* **RODERICK** *curiously.)*

LADY T. Are you acquainted with that gentleman?

FANNY. *(little whimper)* Acquainted. No, Aunt.

LADY T. He appears to have put you out of countenance.

FANNY. *(aside)* Out of countenance? I am transported, my colour rises – my bosom heaves. I shall betray myself...

LADY T. *(suspiciously)* He is a tolerably handsome fellow...

FANNY. *(aside)* Handsome? *(another whimper)* He is my sun, my moon, my love, my life. Yet I darest not speak his name.

LADY T. Niece, if you don't stop that they'll take you away in a cart.

(RODERICK *approaches diffidently.)*

RODERICK. *(bows)* Your servant, ma'am.

LADY T. Do I know you, sir?

RODERICK. I don't have that privilege, my lady, but I understand that bullies and brawlers have entered the tavern and I offer you my protection.

LADY T. That won't be necessary, sir. We are ladies of quality. Our refinement and breeding are our best defence. Still, I thank you. Your name, sir?

(RODERICK *hesitates uneasily.)*

RODERICK. My name is an honourable one though much maligned...

LADY T. But what is it?

RODERICK. It is still a beacon to men of honour.

LADY T. Never mind the beacon – what is your name, sir?

RODERICK. First or second...

LADY T. Your family name.

RODERICK. *(gulps)* Haggard.

(A horse neighs off.)

LADY T. Haggard!

(She picks up a pot and throws it at him.)

RODERICK. *(brightly)* You've heard of me?

LADY T. Yes. You are the young rascal who has pursued Fanny with protestations of affection causing her to be watched day and night.

(BETTY approaches.)

BETTY. Your rooms are ready, ma'am.

LADY T. We shall view them and then dine. In the meantime be gone, sir.

(She exits after BETTY dragging FANNY with her. RODERICK follows protesting.)

(A couple of regular drinkers enter and sit by the fire. These are followed shortly by HAGGARD and GRUNGE.)

(They are now dressed as ONE-EYED WILL and THE HOOK. Hats pulled down, cork moustaches, HAGGARD with an eye patch and a hump, GRUNGE with a hook.)

(They glare about them. The LANDLORD approaches timidly.)

LANDLORD. Sorry, sir, we're about to close.

HAGGARD. You've been granted an extension.

LANDLORD. By whose order?

HAGGARD. By One-eyed Will.

GRUNGE. And The Hook.

(The drinkers move uneasily.)

HAGGARD. *(growls)* Now serve us, damn you or I'll cut your liver out and eat it.

GRUNGE. Aye, brandy by thunder or I'll give you a taste of this.

(He brings the hook crashing down on the table.)

LANDLORD. Yes, sir. At once...

(The LANDLORD hurries off.)

HAGGARD. The table by the fire, Hook.

(He is about to move off. Stops.)

What is it?

GRUNGE. *(struggling)* I've got it stuck.

HAGGARD. *(hisses)* Not again! I told you to be careful.

GRUNGE. *(hisses back)* Why did it have to be the right hand
– I won't be able to unbutton my trousers.

HAGGARD. Just make sure you don't drink too much.

GRUNGE. Couldn't I put a cork on it.

HAGGARD. Certainly not. Do you want everyone to think
you're a pansy, Grunge?

*(He helps to free GRUNGE and they cross to the fire
moving the drinkers out of the way. They sit.)*

*(The LANDLORD and BETTY enter with drinks. They
are shaking so much the glasses rattle on the tray. They
look cautiously away. HAGGARD scowls.)*

What are you staring at?

LANDLORD. Nothing, sir.

HAGGARD. *(erupts)* Nothing! You call this nothing? I lost
this in the service of His Majesty – rot him. And you
call it nothing?

GRUNGE. He's very bitter.

HAGGARD. Of course I'm bitter. Not a penny in
compensation these twenty years – damn your eyes.

LANDLORD. When I said nothing – I meant I wasn't staring...

GRUNGE. Oh, yes, you were. Have you never seen a man
with a hook before?

LANDLORD. Well, yes – but that's a particular fine one, sir.

GRUNGE. *(proudly)* Sheffield steel.

LANDLORD. You can see its quality. Though it must be a
handicap.

GRUNGE. *(fiercely)* Did you say handicap?

LANDLORD. I meant no offence.

HAGGARD. He's very bitter.

GRUNGE. Of course I'm bitter. I shall never be able to play the piano again. They soon forget. We sacrificed our vital organs for those who sleep in silken sheets. We hate the gentry.

HAGGARD. Aye. That's why we burn their ricks and ravish their daughters.

GRUNGE. He's very bitter.

HAGGARD. Of course I'm bitter. That's why we like to see their haughty cheeks grow pale and their silks and satins shake with fear. *(looks around)* In the meantime a song. It's too damned quiet. Sing up, I say.

(The **LANDLORD, BETTY** *and the drinkers begin to sing in quavering tones. Their voices die away as the real* **ONE-EYED WILL** *and* **THE HOOK** *enter the room. They edge out of the room.)*

Louder, damn you!

*(***GRUNGE** *nudges* **HAGGARD**.*)*

*(***HAGGARD** *raises an eye patch to look around. Gives a start.)*

*(***WILL** *and* **THE HOOK** *approach them.)*

WILL. *(silkily)* We thought we'd sit with you, mates – we seem to have more in common...

HAGGARD. Take a berth, shipmates. Have some grog.

WILL. Thankee...

*(***THE HOOK** *continues to glare at* **GRUNGE** *who slips his hook under the table.)*

Members of the Brotherhood?

HAGGARD. Aye.

WILL. I thought so. I'm One-eyed Will and this is The Hook.

HAGGARD. Patch Haggard and Hooky Grunge...

(WILL shakes hands with HAGGARD. THE HOOK extents his hook. GRUNGE eyes it nervously. They shake hooks and become hopelessly entangled. Finally free themselves.)

WILL. *(points to HAGGARD's patch)* Where did you lose yours, mate?

HAGGARD. Off Havana. Caught in a broadside on the old Barracuda.

WILL. One of Flint's men?

HAGGARD. Aye.

WILL. They were hard, were Flint's men. And you, matey?

GRUNGE. The same broadside that took his eye took off my hand. I said 'where's my hand?' He said 'don't expect me to look for it.' How we laughed.

HOOK. *(snarls)* Laughed!

GRUNGE. Only in jest.

HAGGARD. *(hastily)* And you, shipmate?

WILL. Against the Dons. We were took, hanged in chains, lashed and branded – and still we spat on them.

GRUNGE. *(getting carried away)* That was nothing. I was took, lashed, keel hauled, mainbraced and barnacled...

WILL. *(suspiciously)* What?

HAGGARD. *(hastily)* That was nought. I was lashed, thumbscrewed and racked for three days.

WILL. The rack!

HAGGARD. I came out six inches taller and still I spat on them.

GRUNGE. That was nothing – I was hanged.

(They all stare.)

WILL. Hanged? Then how is it that you're alive, my bucko?

GRUNGE. It came on to rain and they all went home. I was cut down by a friendly native. I still can't swallow.

WILL. *(dangerously)* Hook here doesn't believe you. He thinks you're mendicants trying to win sympathy.

HAGGARD. *(blustering)* Mendicants! How do you think he got that, by thunder? It didn't come from biting his nails.

WILL. I'm more interested in your eye, mate. May I see it?

HAGGARD. Well, I don't want to get a cold in it...

(He raises the patch reluctantly.)

WILL. It's very lifelike.

HAGGARD. I thought, have the best.

WILL. See how it glints, Hook.

HOOK. *(peers)* It's bloodshot.

HAGGARD. It's a ruby.

WILL. Show it to me.

(He holds out his hand.)

HAGGARD. I'll have a job getting it back in...

WILL. I'll show you mine if you show me yours...

*(**WILL** removes his eye and lays it on table.)*

*(**HAGGARD** leaps to his feet.)*

What is it?

HAGGARD. Sorry, mates – I suddenly feel three sheets to the wind.

(He exits hurriedly.)

GRUNGE. He hasn't got his land legs yet...

*(**GRUNGE** follows **HAGGARD** out of the door.)*

*(**WILL** and **THE HOOK** roar with laughter.)*

*(Their laughter dies away as **FANNY** and **LADY TARTLET** enter and sit at a far table set for supper. They eye them lecherously.)*

*(**RODERICK** enters and crosses to **WILL** and **THE HOOK**.)*

RODERICK. *(low voice)* You look perfect.

WILL. What?

RODERICK. Absolutely revolting – the pair of you.

WILL. Damn your eyes, do you know who we are?

RODERICK. And the voice – so in character. I've never heard a more unpleasant one.

WILL. *(half rising)* What!

RODERICK. But when are you going to start the ravishing?

WILL. *(stares)* Ravishing.

(He nods towards the ladies.)

RODERICK. We haven't got all night. Get over there before they start eating. Get over there and get on with it.

*(**RODERICK** moves off.)*

*(**WILL** and **THE HOOK** look at each other, shrug, and cross to the ladies.)*

WILL. Ahoy, my dainties.

LADY T. Leave us, sir. We are ladies of quality.

HOOK. We like them best.

LADY T. Desist – we are not your dockside wenches.

WILL. *(bows)* Allow us some delicacy, ma'am. First a glass of wine. *(he takes a glass)* Then we'll dance a measure...

HOOK. And then the ravishing...

FANNY. Help! Will no one save us?

*(**RODERICK** bounds back into the room.)*

RODERICK. Have no fear, Fanny – Roderick's here. You have my protection.

*(**WILL** and **HOOK** stare at him in astonishment.)*

Leave, sir – before I close your other eye – and tell your friend with the surgical appliance to do the same.

HOOK. *(puzzled)* But I thought this was your –

*(Before he can finish **RODERICK** has seized him by the throat, shakes him up and down, stamps on him, picks him up and throws him out the door.)*

WILL. *(gasps)* You've done that to The Hook?

RODERICK. And I'll serve you the same, you dastardly cur. *(points at door)* Now, go.

(**WILL** *hesitates then looks cowered and slinks away just as* **HAGGARD** *has described.*)

FANNY. My hero.

(*She falls into his arms.*)

(**LADY TARTLET** *separates them.*)

LADY T. How can we thank you, sir?

RODERICK. It was nothing.

LADY T. My brother will hear of this. You must dine with us.

RODERICK. A pleasure, ma'am.

LADY T. In the meantime, Fanny is near to swooning.

FANNY. (*whispers*) I must loosen my stays, aunt.

LADY T. We must retire and recover ourselves. Afterwards you may join us at our table.

(*The ladies exit,*)

RODERICK. Oh, happy day.

(**HAGGARD** *and* **GRUNGE** *poke their heads around the door.*)

HAGGARD. Have they gone?

RODERICK. Who?

HAGGARD. One-eyed Will and the Hook.

RODERICK. Look, don't come back in here – you'll spoil – (*stops*) One-eyed Will...

GRUNGE. And The Hook. They've just been in here...

RODERICK. (*totters*) You mean...they were...they were the real...

GRUNGE. One-eyed Will and The Hook.

RODERICK. And I...

HAGGARD. Put them to flight. Don't faint now, Roderick. The birds have flown. And you are a hero. It was a brilliant stratagem.

(*Sounds of chanting off.*)

What's that hullabaloo, Grunge?

(GRUNGE crosses to window.)

GRUNGE. There's an angry mob outside. They've assembled a barrel of oil, a pile of feathers, and a long pole...

HAGGARD. What are they chanting?

GRUNGE. Tar and feather them and ride them out of town.

HAGGARD. They don't mean us, surely.

GRUNGE. They're waving their fists.

RODERICK. *(looks around)* And there's no one here but you and Grunge...

HAGGARD. It's our disguise – once we reveal ourselves they'll be amused at the jest. Come, Grunge.

(They cross to the window. They remove their hats, wipe off their moustaches. HAGGARD removes his eye patch and GRUNGE his hook. They wave.)

(There is a gasp from the mob.)

(The chanting begins again.)

What are they chanting now, Grunge?

GRUNGE. Tar and feather them and ride them out of town.

(They all stare at each other and dash for the door.)

(Curtain)

Scene Three – The Great Lover

(The Tartlets' london house. Evening.)

*(**LADY TARTLET**'s withdrawing room. The room has the appearance of a boudoir. Chaise-longue, tables and chairs, drinks tray. On the wall a fierce picture of **LORD TARTLET**.)*

(Doors off, stage right and left. Downstage left are french windows.)

(Noises off, voices, laughter, clink of glasses.)

*(**FANNY** enters breathlessly followed by **RODERICK**. He embraces her.)*

FANNY. Roderick, you must not.

RODERICK. *(ardently)* Must not?

FANNY. Follow me here. This is my aunt's boudoir. She would not approve of us being here alone.

RODERICK. But your aunt favours me.

FANNY. But not my father. He will not hear of our engagement. I am to marry the son of a brewer with fifty thousand a year.

RODERICK. Then may he drown in his own vat, the dog.

FANNY. What is to be done, Roderick?

RODERICK. We must elope.

FANNY. Elope!

(She moves downstage.)

I am transported.

RODERICK. We must elope tonight.

FANNY. Tonight!

(She becomes busy with the fan.)

But it cannot be. My aunt occupies the adjoining chamber and is a light sleeper. And Lord Tartlet is confined to the ground floor with gout, dropsy and the windy spasms.

RODERICK. Even so we must risk all, Fanny.

FANNY. Oh, foolish youth. When I saw you across the room tonight nervously fingering your pommel I knew you planned some desperate act.

RODERICK. Tonight, Fanny – we shall enter the gates of ecstasy.

FANNY. That's done it.

(She sits.)

But, Roderick, how can we enter the gates of ecstasy when my aunt sits before them like the gorgon?

RODERICK. Tonight Perseus shall slay the gorgon.

FANNY. You, Roderick?

RODERICK. Not I. Longstock the poet will slay the gorgon – not with a sword but with honeyed words and blandishments.

FANNY. Longstock! In truth she has talked of no one else since she met him. Is he here?

RODERICK. He is out there now.

(Laughter off.)

Amusing the company with his bon mots and amusing sallies.

FANNY. I can't wait to meet him, although I must confess I've read nothing he's written.

RODERICK. You won't – he hasn't written anything.

FANNY. What?

RODERICK. But you have met him. *(lowers voice)* Longstock is my father.

FANNY. *(stares)* It is a stratagem.

RODERICK. Indeed. You must place a few simple possessions in a bag and drop them from your chamber window – then emerge as though taking the night air. In the meantime Longstock will divert Lady Tartlet.

FANNY. Roderick, this is madness. Lord Tartlet has spies everywhere; even those eyes in the portrait seem to follow me about the room.

RODERICK. That's the sign of a good portrait when the eyes follow you about the room – there's nothing to be afraid of, Fanny.

FANNY. But Lord Tartlet can be violently jealous and he has a short way with rivals.

RODERICK. How so?

FANNY. He has them beaten by ruffians, put in a sack and thrown from Tower Bridge.

RODERICK. Fear not – my father intends to charm the old fool. Now go and prepare...

(*He follows her to the door.*)

FANNY. No, stay – we must not be seen together...

(*She exits leaving* **RODERICK** *alone in the room. He studies the portrait moving this way and that to see if the eyes follow him.* **LADY TARTLET** *enters the room followed by* **HAGGARD.** **HAGGARD** *is dressed soberly with a flowing necktie.*)

LADY T. Tish! You go too far, sir.

(*Taps him with her fan.*)

But I must say you are vastly amusing.

(*She sees* **RODERICK.**)

Roderick, what are you doing here?

RODERICK. (*smoothly*) Looking for you, Lady Tartlet. But stay, am I in the presence of Longstock the poet?

HAGGARD. (*modestly*) You are, sir.

RODERICK. At last. I've long been an admirer of your work, sir.

HAGGARD. You're too kind.

RODERICK. Pray, may I stay for a moment and listen to the gems of your conversation?

HAGGARD. I'm afraid not – my conversation is private.

RODERICK. Then I'll withdraw. Your servant.

HAGGARD. And yours.

(**RODERICK** *bows and exits.*)

The price of fame, I'm afraid.

LADY T. *(studies him)* And yet strange that I've never read a book of yours or even heard of you – nor have the booksellers.

HAGGARD. My poems are in private circulation, ma'am – and my books are under a pseudonym. I'm sure you've read *My Secret Life* by A Gentleman.

LADY T. *(shocked) My Secret Life!* But that's pornographic.

HAGGARD. Pornography raised to high art ma'am.

LADY T. *(dimpling)* Well, I must say the scene in the sedan chair was well written but was it believable?

HAGGARD. Believable?

LADY T. The incident between the Countess and Walter. Even if it were physically possible would she have yielded so readily to someone who had merely enquired the way to Blackheath?

HAGGARD. You're forgetting – the Countess was Italian, ma'am and had previously worked as a contortionist in a circus.

LADY T. But what of Walter? Is he believable?

HAGGARD. You are looking at him...

LADY T. Then I'm in danger.

HAGGARD. No, I'm the one in danger, ma'am.

(He moves closer.)

Your hair that would bind me with silken threads...your teeth as white as the coral that would snare the unwary sailor...the smooth peaks that tempt the climber to even greater heights.

LADY T. You go too far, sir.

HAGGARD. Not far enough, dear lady. We should seize the moment. 'For life is short – and death is worse. The grave is silent – do worms converse?'

LADY T. A poem.

HAGGARD. For you. Reward me with a kiss from those ruby lips.

LADY T. Stay, sir. My husband is a jealous man. Have you noticed how those eyes seem to follow you around the room?

HAGGARD. Then later – I shall come to you.

LADY T. Later then. But be circumspect – my husband misses nothing. Now I must attend to my guests. *(listens)* I believe Lord Chesterfield has arrived.

(She crosses.)

No, stay – he must not see us together...

(She exits.)

*(**HAGGARD** pours himself a drink. Studies portrait. He moves around to see if the eyes follow him.)*

(Tap on the french window.)

*(He admits **GRUNGE**, again somberly dressed.)*

HAGGARD. What were you doing out there?

GRUNGE. Getting cold.

HAGGARD. You should be mingling. Do you have pad and pencil?

GRUNGE. Yes, sir – but what am I supposed to do?

HAGGARD. You are my Boswell. All great literary figures have them. You'll note down my sayings – that's if you can spell them. My epigrams, *bon mots*, repartees and amusing sallies.

GRUNGE. That'll be the day.

HAGGARD. What was that, Grunge?

GRUNGE. A drink, sir?

HAGGARD. Not too much. I must keep a clear head, for tonight I worship at the temple of Aphrodite.

GRUNGE. *(pouring)* I didn't know we were going to church.

HAGGARD. I was referring to Lady Tartlet. By midnight I shall be enjoying the felicities of her person. Don't try and spell that, Grunge.

GRUNGE. Take care, sir. Remember what happened to Lord Effingham...

HAGGARD. The champion hurdler?

GRUNGE. Until his tragic accident... He was enjoying the felicities of her person. They found him in a sack on Hampstead Heath...

(**RODERICK** *enters furtively.*)

HAGGARD. Ah, Roderick – is all prepared?

RODERICK. Yes, but Fanny is afraid her aunt will discover all.

HAGGARD. I've taken care of that. Tonight I shall create a diversion. I shall seduce Lady Tartlet

(**RODERICK** *and* **GRUNGE** *exchange grins.*)

Have I said something amusing? She's a lusty woman married to an invalid husband. I see no problem.

RODERICK. There is one. Lord Tartlet. He's a man to be feared. Don't forget what happened to Lord Effingham.

HAGGARD. The champion hurdler?

RODERICK. Not anymore. They say he's never been astride a horse since.

GRUNGE. Nor anything else for that matter.

RODERICK. His regenerative powers were damaged beyond repair.

HAGGARD. He'll have to catch me first. In my youth I was famed for my lightning seductions. I once seduced Lady Dalrymple between the cheese and biscuits and the fruit and nuts – and Lord Dalrymple was none the wiser. Now, is all arranged?

RODERICK. Yes, the coach waits at the back door but there is danger. There are footmen patrolling the grounds.

HAGGARD. Then make sure Grunge has sword and pistol to cover your retreat.

GRUNGE. And who's going to cover my retreat?

HAGGARD. I shall.

GRUNGE. I thought you were covering Lady Tartlet.

HAGGARD. That's enough, Grunge. You are talking of your betters.

GRUNGE. That's not what I've heard.

HAGGARD. I don't care what you've heard. And don't worry about Lord Tartlet, Roderick. He'll not wake tonight for the same reason Lord Dalrymple didn't wake...

(He holds up bottle.)

Laudanum.

(He picks up glass.)

I give you Lady Tartlet. As fine a woman who ever drew on stays. Whose beauty is only exceeded by her generosity. And Lord Tartlet who has proved an equally generous host – the old dotard...

(They laugh then become aware that **LORD TARTLET** *has entered the room.)*

(He is a severe looking man in his sixties with a heavily bandaged foot. He is accompanied by **LORD CHESTERFIELD**, *a pompous, heavy man,* **LADY TARTLET** *and* **FANNY**.)

LADY T. Ah, Longstock, may I present you to Lord Tartlet...

HAGGARD. Your servant, sir.

*(***HAGGARD*** moves forward and treads on* **LORD TARTLET***s foot. Groan.)*

LORD T. You have stood on my foot, sir.

HAGGARD. My deepest apologies. I'm afraid I've injured your father.

LADY T. *(flattered)* Not my father – my husband.

HAGGARD. *(kindly)* You must have suffered a great deal, sir.

LORD T. I suffer from gout, that is all.

LADY T. His Lordship is sensitive on the subject.

HAGGARD. Then he should be bled twice a day, fed on lentils, and kept off this accursed stuff.

*(***HAGGARD*** pours himself a large measure.)*

Otherwise your wife will continue to look twenty years younger.

LADY T. I am twenty years younger. I'm his Lordship's second wife. His first marriage was not a happy one.

HAGGARD. I see. Well, to marry once may be considered a mistake but to marry twice is the triumph of hope over experience.

(Murmurs of appreciation.)

GRUNGE. Brilliant. *(makes a note.)*

LORD C. Didn't Dr Johnson say that?

HAGGARD. Not yet – but he will.

LADY T. Lord Chesterfield, may I present Longstock, the poet.

(**LORD CHESTERFIELD** *regards him suspiciously and takes a pinch of snuff.*)

LORD C. A poet, you say?

HAGGARD. I've scribbled a few lines that are not without merit.

LORD C. Never heard of you.

HAGGARD. Really? My Ode to an Expiring Chaffinch has been much admired.

LORD C. And now I suppose you're looking for a patron.

HAGGARD. Indeed not. For what is a patron but a man who supports with insolence and is rewarded by flattery.

(Murmurs of appreciation.)

GRUNGE. Very apt. *(makes another note.)*

LORD C. What?

LADY T. You must not tease Lord Chesterfield, Longstock.

LORD C. It is of no consequence, ma'am. A fly may sting a noble horse but in the end the fly is still an insect whilst the horse is still noble.

(Murmurs of appreciation.)

(**GRUNGE** *makes a reluctant note.*)

LADY T. You see, Lord Chesterfield is a great wit, Longstock.

HAGGARD. So I understand – I was told he was a lord amongst wits...now I find he's merely a wit amongst lords.

(A gasp of appreciation.)

GRUNGE. That's put the lid on it.

(He makes another note.)

*(**LORD CHESTERFIELD** moves off.)*

LORD C. Bah!

*(**LORD CHESTERFIELD** exits followed by **LORD TARTLET**.)*

LORD T. Chesterfield...

LADY T. Longstock, you have insulted Lord Chesterfield.

HAGGARD. How can you insult someone who's named after a sofa?

*(**LADY TARTLET** follows the company out.)*

HAGGARD. Quick, you two. Onto the terrace and wait for Fanny to drop her reticule...

*(He ushers them out of the french windows. **LADY TARTLET** returns.)*

*(**HAGGARD** takes her in his arms.)*

LADY T. I cannot stay long. His Lordship suspects.

HAGGARD. Forgive me – I cannot control my amorous propensities. A glimpse of that white bosom has enflamed me.

LADY T. No!

HAGGARD. Later, then.

LADY. But what of my husband?

HAGGARD. It would take him half an hour to mount the stairs. Besides, I laugh at danger.

LADY T. Lord Effington laughed at danger – now he seldom goes forth without a nurse...

(The door to the drawing room opens slightly and
HAGGARD *catches a glimpse of a bandaged foot poking*
through.)

HAGGARD. *(louder voice)* And the dog deserved it.

LADY T. *(stares)* What?

HAGGARD. Now I must withdraw. Your reputation and that
of his Lordship are too dear to me to risk gossip and
slander. In fact I'm composing a verse in his honour
– once I've found a word to rhyme with Tartlet. It
begins, 'Oh noble Tartlet, champion of freedom and
defender of the weak who limps with bandaged foot
through halls of fame...'

*(**LORD TARTLET** enters glowering.)*

LORD T. *(coldly)* Would you attend to your guests my
dear? I'll entertain Mr Longstock...

LADY T. Yes, husband...

(She exits.)

HAGGARD. Allow me to assist you to a chair – I can see your
foot is painful this evening...

LORD T. *(sits)* A minor irritation. Don't underestimate my
vigour, Longstock. Lord Effington made that mistake.

*(**HAGGARD** pours them drinks.)*

HAGGARD. Ah, Lord Effington, the champion hurdler.

LORD T. But not anymore – they say he can barely clear a
kerb these days...

HAGGARD. Even so, I have here a sovereign cure for gout.
(produces bottle.)

LORD T. A cure for gout?

HAGGARD. My father's own remedy. He once took this, rose
from a bed of pain and walked five miles to a hanging.

LORD T. *(smiles)* Why not?

*(**HAGGARD** adds the drug to the drink.)*

Oh, Longstock, would you close the window, I feel a
draught...

HAGGARD. Certainly.

*(He crosses. **LORD TARTLET** reverses the glasses. **HAGGARD** hears them clink.)*

(They are about to drink.)

HAGGARD. *(starts)* That picture!

LORD T. What?

HAGGARD. I swear I saw the eyes blink.

LORD T. They say that's the sign of a good picture – when the eyes appear to blink... *(he turns)*

*(**HAGGARD** reverses the glasses. **LORD TARTLET** hears him.)*

Fetch me a cushion would you, Longstock.

HAGGARD. Certainly...

*(He fetches the cushion. This time **LORD TARTLET** merely clinks the glasses.)*

(They are about to drink.)

HAGGARD. It's doing it again!

*(**LORD TARTLET** turns. **HAGGARD** reverses the glasses.)*

LORD T. It is a most animated picture...

HAGGARD. Your health, your Lordship...

*(**HAGGARD** drinks deep.)*

LORD T. And yours, Haggard.

*(**LORD TARTLET** drinks deep.)*

HAGGARD. Haggard? I fear you are mistaken, my lord.

LORD T. No, I've had you watched day and night. Your name is not Longstock. You planned to seduce my wife and make off with my niece Fanny.

HAGGARD. There's some mistake.

LORD T. And you've made it, Haggard. Do you know what I'm going to do? I shall summon the servants, have you beaten, put in a sack and thrown into the Thames.

HAGGARD. Too late, Tartlet, too late. You'll never reach the bell rope...

LORD T. What?

HAGGARD. Feeling drowsy? Are your limbs like lead?

LORD T. No.

HAGGARD. They will be. In a moment you will lapse into a deep coma...

*(**HAGGARD**'s voice becomes slower.)*

And I shall be gone – like a will-o-the-wisp.

*(**HAGGARD** begins to sound like a run-down gramophone.)*

LORD T. Your voice grows drowsy, Haggard.

HAGGARD. That's the effect of the drug. You'll find everything appears to move in slow motion...

(He moves off like a slow motion film.)

And I shall be gone...like a phantom...fleeter than Mercury...

(He reaches the door to drawing room.)

Farewell, Tartlet, farewell...

(He exits. Loud crash off.)

*(**LORD TARTLET** smiles and follows closing the door.)*

*(**GRUNGE** enters through french windows as **RODERICK** enters from the back.)*

GRUNGE. Is all ready, Master Roderick?

RODERICK. Aye, the horses are champing at the bit – and so am I. You remember the plan, Grunge?

GRUNGE. Yes. While the squire romances Lady Tartlet the clock strikes twelve Miss Fanny drops a bag containing a few simple possessions from her chamber window then emerges to take the night air...

(Crash from the terrace.)

RODERICK. What was that?

(They cross to the window.)

GRUNGE. There's a large sack on the terrace. If they're a few simple possessions – she's taking the wardrobe!

RODERICK. It's moving, Grunge.

GRUNGE. And groaning... You don't think she got it wrong and she's dropped from the window?

RODERICK. And her simple possessions come out of the door? Don't be a fool, Grunge.

GRUNGE. It's got up! It's coming towards us!

(They stand back.)

*(**HAGGARD** hops through the french windows. Only his head protrudes from the sack.)*

HAGGARD. *(shouts)* Out the back!

(He hops across the room as though in a sack race.)

(The others follow.)

(Curtain)

Scene Four – Forbidden Fruit

(Haggard Hall. An evening before Christmas. **HAGGARD** *is sitting at a long table by the fire. He is doing his accounts. Two things distract him: the sound of carol singers and the presence of a large trunk in the corner.)*

HAGGARD. *(calls)* Grunge!

*(**GRUNGE** enters.)*

GRUNGE. Sir?

HAGGARD. Why has this trunk been left here?

GRUNGE. Master Roderick had the men bring it in.

HAGGARD. It can't stay here.

(He gestures at the dust and debris of the room.)

I have the room tastefully arranged for Christmas.

GRUNGE. The men said it was too heavy to take upstairs.

HAGGARD. The lazy dogs.

(The carol singers reach a crescendo.)

Are the pennies heated for the carol singers, Grunge?

GRUNGE. Piping hot, sir.

HAGGARD. Good.

(He takes a small shovel from the fire)

They can't say we don't give them a warm welcome at Haggard Hall.

(He throws the coins out through the window. The singing breaks off. Cries of "God bless you, Sir.")

Don't let them burn a hole in your pockets…

SINGERS. *(off)* 'We wish ou a merry Christmas and a happy –

(The singing breaks off in cries of pain. Cries of "Hell fire!" "You swine!" and "Poxy knave!" waft through the window.)

*(**HAGGARD** shakes his head.)*

HAGGARD. They never see the funny side.

(**RODERICK** *enters with two glasses of wine. He crosses and reclines on the trunk.*)

Two glasses, Roderick?

RODERICK. It is Christmas, father.

(**BETTY BOUNCER** *enters from the hall.* **HAGGARD** *turns in surprise.* **RODERICK** *seizes the opportunity to pass one glass into the trunk.*)

HAGGARD. Betty! What are you doing here?

BETTY. I was sent for.

HAGGARD. By whom?

BETTY. Master Roderick.

HAGGARD. What!

RODERICK. *(hesitates)* I can explain, father.

HAGGARD. One moment – is this my Christmas present?

RODERICK. I can't afford a Christmas present.

BETTY. *(reproachfully)* I didn't come for money…

HAGGARD. Of course not. Roderick.

BETTY. I'm a good girl.

HAGGARD. Indeed. *(about to speak)*

BETTY. Virtue is its own reward.

HAGGARD. Yes. What I want to know –

BETTY. Above rubies…

HAGGARD. Will you stop blathering? If we can't afford to employ her what is she doing here?

RODERICK. I'm getting married.

HAGGARD. What!!

(**BETTY** *moves downstage.*)

BETTY. Oh, joy. The answer to my dreams. I shall be a lady.

HAGGARD. You can't marry a serving wench.

BETTY. He doesn't care. My modest nature and quiet good looks have captivated him…

RODERICK. I'm not marrying this baggage. No offence, Betty.

BETTY. *(curtsy)* None taken, sir.

HAGGARD. Then who is it? You seem loath to say.

BETTY. I think I know, sir. Fanny Foulacre has been abducted...

HAGGARD. Fanny Foulacre!

GRUNGE. The whole county is in uproar...

(They all stare at the trunk.)

*(**HAGGARD** crosses to the trunk, raises the lid and closes it abruptly.)*

HAGGARD. It's Fanny Foulacre!

RODERICK. I thought Betty could be bridesmaid.

BETTY. Always the bridesmaid – never the bride...

HAGGARD. Why such haste, Roderick? Does she have a bun on the griddle?

RODERICK. Certainly not. But the dissenters say it's the end of the world on Friday and it doesn't leave much time for the honeymoon.

HAGGARD. End of the world. I must remember to put on a clean shirt. Surely, you don't believe that rabble.

GRUNGE. There's a reason for it.

HAGGARD. What reason?

GRUNGE. They say it's punishment due to the outbreak of fornication, lust and lechery...

HAGGARD. It's not broken out around here. I'd have noticed.

GRUNGE. *(darkly)* Not yet...

*(**HAGGARD** leads **RODERICK** downstage.)*

HAGGARD. *(low voice)* Roderick, Fanny's father is the most powerful man in the county. He could ruin us.

RODERICK. He's also as rich as parliament. And she's the apple of his eye.

HAGGARD. He is also an unforgiving man and a canting Methodist.

RODERICK. But once we're married...

HAGGARD. *(leads* **RODERICK** *further away from* **GRUNGE** *and* **BETTY***)* Marriage? The vicar won't marry you. We've taken his glebe land.

RODERICK. Then we must give it back.

HAGGARD. We can't – we've sold it. No, the ceremony must be carried out by an unfrocked priest in the Haggard crypt – in total secrecy...

(He turns to see **GRUNGE** *listening. Loud knocking on the outer door.)*

Well, don't just stand there, Grunge.

*(***GRUNGE** *exits.)*

(The lid of the trunk begins to open. **RODERICK** *and* **HAGGARD** *hurry to close it. They sit on it as* **GRUNGE** *enters with* **SIR JOSH FOULACRE***.)*

GRUNGE. Sir Josh Foulacre.

SIR JOSH. Your servant, Haggard.

HAGGARD. And yours, sir.

SIR JOSH. I'm looking for my daughter.

HAGGARD. *(quickly)* She's not here.

SIR JOSH. I should hope not – for she's been abducted.

HAGGARD. Abducted!

SIR JOSH. As a magistrate I thought you may have been aware of the fact – even had knowledge of her whereabouts...

(He looks around suspiciously.)

HAGGARD. Where was she last seen?

SIR JOSH. At the turnpike. She was seen talking to a young man of villainous appearance. He was in charge of a wagon and appeared to be transporting a large trunk...

HAGGARD. *(guiding* **SIR JOSH** *hurriedly to the door)* Be assured, sir – I shall be vigilant. Where may I reach you?

SIR JOSH. I've taken a room at The Swan With Two Necks – you may reach me there.

(He turns at the door.)

SIR JOSH. She's my only daughter and very dear to me. I shall not rest. I shall hound the scoundrel to the quarries, to the hulks, to transportation. Even then I shall hound him until he longs for death.

HAGGARD. It's the end of the world on Friday.

SIR JOSH. Then he shall pray for it. For the wrath of God will not be as terrible as mine. *(bows)* Your servant.

*(**GRUNGE** sees him out.)*

HAGGARD. That's torn it. We must act quickly, Roderick. Install her in the tower room and make her yours tonight.

RODERICK. But what of the ceremony?

HAGGARD. There'll be no ceremony – not with Sir Josh on the rampage. But once she's yours he'll agree to the match.

*(**GRUNGE** returns.)*

GRUNGE. *(firmly)* No. Not without the benefit of clergy.

HAGGARD. What!

GRUNGE. Do you know where I sleep tonight?

HAGGARD. Where you always sleep. In the stable to keep my horse warm.

GRUNGE. Not tonight. Tonight I shall lie at her door like the faithful hound. And none shall assail her honour.

HAGGARD. Don't come beating your tambourine around here, Grunge. You'll do as you're told.

RODERICK. But if he talks...

(They confer.)

HAGGARD. Very well, Grunge – you may sleep at her door. Roderick only wants what's best for Fanny. *(aside)* You can always step over him. What else can we do?

*(**BETTY** enters.)*

BETTY. *(primly)* I've already done it. I've sent for the vicar.

GRUNGE. Well done, Betty.

(The **VICAR** *enters.)*

(He is a vinegary looking man in his forties.)

VICAR. I've come at the urgent request of your servants, Haggard – to save the good name of a young lady...

GRUNGE. Praise be.

HAGGARD. *(frowns)* We were just going to send for you, vicar.

RODERICK. This very minute.

VICAR. It will mean the return of the glebe.

*(***HAGGARD** *and* **RODERICK** *exchange glances.)*

HAGGARD. But of course...

VICAR. And where is the bride?

*(***HAGGARD** *and* **RODERICK** *raise the lid of the trunk.* **FANNY** *emerges.)*

(She is wearing a bridal dress and holding a veil. They stare.)

FANNY. I thought I'd change whilst I was waiting...

(She reaches into the trunk and takes out a wedding cake, a 'just married' sign and confetti. These items are followed by a small pageboy. **HAGGARD** *peers in the trunk.)*

HAGGARD. No choir?

RODERICK. As you see, vicar – we practise nothing underhand.

HAGGARD. Indeed not. Tonight there'll be dancing in the great hall. Tune the spinet, Grunge, and send for the blind fiddler.

VICAR. And where is the ceremony to take place?

HAGGARD. Why not here? We'd prefer a quiet wedding.

FANNY. *(disdainfully)* Will there be dusting?

HAGGARD. Dusting?

FANNY. See – I can write my name in the dust...

(She writes. **HAGGARD** *looks on admiringly.)*

HAGGARD. Yes... Isn't education a wonderful thing. Grunge, dust the furniture, wash the crystal, polish the silver and beat the curtains.

(GRUNGE exits muttering.)

GRUNGE. Stick a broom up my backside I'll sweep the floor as well...

VICAR. *(considers)* There should be witnesses...

HAGGARD. Betty, summon the servants – and here's the key to the wine cellar. Tonight we'll celebrate with a wild carouse.

FANNY. Not too wild, I hope. I've heard that your routs can get out of hand. That a cat was thrown from a window and the guests so drunk they could barely stand.

HAGGARD. A gross exaggeration. We wouldn't ill-treat a poor dumb animal. It was the cat who could barely stand and a guest who was thrown from the window.

FANNY. I also heard that you rode a horse through the ladies' bedrooms, Roderick.

RODERICK. The horse was blinkered, Fanny.

(BETTY enters with a surly bunch of servants.)

(HAGGARD whispers to RODERICK.)

HAGGARD. You can tell when they haven't had their Christmas box...

(They assemble.)

VICAR. *(rapidly)* Dearly beloved, we are gathered in the sight of God and in the face of this congregation to join this man and this woman in holy matrimony...

(His voice dies away as a young woman enters from the hall carrying a baby in a small crib which she thrusts into RODERICK's arms. The baby begins to cry.)

(The young woman runs from the room.)

FANNY. Roderick! How could you?

(She dashes after the young woman. The congregation follows.)

HAGGARD. Grunge, lock the outer door – make sure no one leaves…

(**RODERICK** *places the crib on the table.*)

HAGGARD. Well, sir?

RODERICK. It's not mine.

(**HAGGARD** *remains silent.*)

RODERICK. Don't you believe me?

HAGGARD. Roderick, I have a blunderbuss that spreads less shot than you.

RODERICK. It doesn't even look like me.

HAGGARD. I must say, it doesn't look like a Haggard.

(**HAGGARD** *opens the door.*)

Grunge, send in the girl…

(The girl enters looking sulky.)

What's your name, my child?

NELLY. Nelly. Nelly Blight.

HAGGARD. What a delightful name. Now I want you to tell the truth, Nelly, and shame the devil. That child is not a Haggard.

RODERICK. He looks more like a monkey.

NELLY. You mean he's not good enough for you. You've had your fun but what about my shame? It's the rich what gets the pleasure – it's the poor what gets the blame.

RODERICK. But I'm not the one what's had the pleasure – who's had the pleasure.

HAGGARD. Come, tell us the truth.

NELLY. *(ambiguously)* It's a gentleman what done this to me and a gentleman what will pay.

HAGGARD. And so he shall. But who done it to you – did it to you?

NELLY. It was dark and he wore a brimmed hat. He said he was a gentleman.

HAGGARD. He may have been a gentleman. He was not a Haggard. A Haggard would have removed his hat under those circumstances.

NELLY. He said he was a Haggard. He promised me a life of riches, of silks and satins and golden guineas. He said he had great expectations and then…

HAGGARD. Yes?

NELLY. He done it – and it was me who had the expectations.

HAGGARD. Is there nothing else you can tell us?

NELLY. Only that he could talk the hind leg off a donkey. He'd take my hands, rough from honest toil, and say he could see a time when electric fluid would drive machines and wash our clothes and dishes – and dry them. And we would sit all day like ladies and have sherry parties…

(**HAGGARD**'s eyes narrow.)

HAGGARD. Roderick, look at the child. Who does he remind you of?

RODERICK. Grunge!

HAGGARD. He has the same idiotic expression.

RODERICK. And see the way he blows bubbles from his mouth?

HAGGARD. I've seen Grunge do that often.

RODERICK. And he often wears a wide brimmed hat.

HAGGARD. (shouts) Grunge!

(**GRUNGE** enters timidly.)

(**HAGGARD** takes a hat from a peg and thrusts it down firmly on **GRUNGE**'s head.)

NELLY. That's him!

HAGGARD. You're getting married, Grunge. Roderick take Nelly to Fanny – ask her to prepare Nelly for a wedding. You can be next.

(RODERICK leads NELLY out.)

GRUNGE. But, sir –

HAGGARD. She'll look lovely in a veil. I'll wager you can hardly wait. And you may wear my second best coat…

(He thrusts GRUNGE into his coat. Stands back admiringly)

My word. You certainly pay for dressing, Grunge.

GRUNGE. But, sir – I can't go through with it. I know I've transgressed but there was another – she told me so – a proper gentleman –

HAGGARD. Grunge, I'm a magistrate. If you don't maintain the child the parish must and that means prison for you. Would you prefer to spend the night in the arms of Venus or a cold prison cell?

GRUNGE. A cold prison cell.

HAGGARD. We can't afford any scandal, Grunge. If you go through with this I shall buy you…your own pie shop.

GRUNGE. *(tempted)* Pie shop.

HAGGARD. Think – as many pies as you can eat, you glutton.

(The VICAR enters followed by the rest of the wedding party.)

VICAR. Are we having a wedding or not?

HAGGARD. *(pushes grunge forward)* Not one – but two.

VICAR. I don't like this, Haggard. I thought it was strange when there were no banns, no father, and the bride arrived in a trunk but now this – I think I must withdraw...

HAGGARD. Aren't you forgetting the glebe…?

VICAR. *(sighs)* Very well, Who's to be best man?

HAGGARD. Now, Grunge there's something you must decide and whatever you decide will hurt one of us. Is it to be Roderick or myself?

GRUNGE. I can't go through with it.

HAGGARD. He's chosen me, vicar.

(He pushes **GRUNGE** *alongside* **NELLY** *who coyly drops her veil.)*

Ravishing. Think, Grunge, last night you slept beside my horse – tonight you'll be as near to heaven as the man who rides the air balloon at Vauxhall.

GRUNGE. I can't stand heights –

HAGGARD. *(grips Grunge firmly)* We're ready.

VICAR. *(rapidly)* Dearly beloved, we are gathered here in the sight of God and in the face of this congregation to join this man and this woman in holy matrimony. Therefore if any man can show just cause why they may not be lawfully joined let him speak now or forever hold his peace...

*(***GRUNGE*** looks around hopefully.)*

GRUNGE. Did somebody say something?

VICAR. No.

GRUNGE. Would you repeat it – I didn't quite catch it.

VICAR. It wasn't meant for you.

GRUNGE. It is my wedding.

VICAR. *(sighs and gabbles)* ...just cause why they may not be joined together let him speak now or forever hold his peace –

(The door swings open and **SIR JOSH** *enters sword in hand.)*

SIR JOSH. I am that man. I come here to expose that knave and brand him a vile seducer who has ensnared my daughter with blandishments and traps.

(He seizes **GRUNGE** *by the scruff of the neck.)*

Now I come like the hound from hell to wreak vengeance. I shall take the dog out of this house and slay him.

GRUNGE. Sanctuary!

*(***NELLY*** screams.)*

*(***SIR JOSH*** turns to **NELLY**.)*

SIR JOSH. And as for you, miss – remove that livery of Satan that has brought disgrace upon your father and your name and let me see the shame behind that veil…

(He pulls back the veil. He staggers back at the sight of **NELLY**.*)*

NELLY. Josh!

SIR JOSH. Nelly!

FANNY. Father?

*(***NELLY** *takes the crib from* **FANNY** *and thrusts it into* **SIR JOSH***'s arms.)*

SIR JOSH. Fanny!

FANNY. *(reproachfully)* Father.

(She dashes from the room.)

*(***SIR JOSH** *follows still holding the baby.)*

NELLY. Josh!

(She follows him.)

(Silence.)

(The **VICAR** *brings his book down on* **GRUNGE**'s *head and storms out.* **GRUNGE** *collapses senseless.)*

(Curtain)

End of Act One

ACT TWO

Scene One – Unclean

(The Swan With Two Necks. Christmas Eve. Carol singers outside.)

(HAGGARD and RODERICK are drinking by the fire. A PREACHER and a SEAFARING MAN are eating at an adjacent table.)

(GRUNGE enters and stands by the table.)

HAGGARD. What is it, Grunge?

GRUNGE. Sir Josh Foulacre is outside in his carriage. He wishes to make arrangements for tomorrow.

HAGGARD. What does he plan for tomorrow?

GRUNGE. Your death.

HAGGARD. What!

GRUNGE. He says you've insulted him and demands satisfaction.

LANDLORD. Did you say Sir Josh?

HAGGARD. Yes.

LANDLORD. He's the finest shot in three counties.

GRUNGE. Never misses.

LANDLORD. He's killed three men in duels.

GRUNGE. And there's one who'll never walk again.

HAGGARD. And do you think I'd insult such a man?

RODERICK. You did.

HAGGARD. Did I?

RODERICK. He said you called him a cross-grained cur and a posturing braggart.

HAGGARD. Who told him that?

RODERICK. I did. I said you were as good a man as he. And you've never lost a duel.

HAGGARD. That's because I cheat, Roderick.

RODERICK. He's afraid of you, father.

HAGGARD. *(crosses to window)* Are you sure?

RODERICK. That's why he's cowering in his carriage, and his death will mean I'll be free to marry Fanny.

HAGGARD. I thought that was off.

RODERICK. It's on again.

(**HAGGARD** *takes hand bell from table and rings it.* **BETTY** *enters.*)

HAGGARD. Ah, Betty – is Sir Josh out there in his carriage?

BETTY. Yes, sir.

HAGGARD. Is he afraid to come in?

BETTY. Yes, sir.

RODERICK. You see, father – he fears you.

BETTY. Sir Josh is afraid of no man. He's killed five in duels.

HAGGARD. I thought it was three.

BETTY. Three with pistols – two with swords.

GRUNGE. And there is one who'll never walk again.

HAGGARD. Will you stop saying that. Then why is he afraid?

BETTY. He's been afraid since Amos Bindweed died from a putrefaction of the inward parts. He fears the plague…

HAGGARD. The plague!

(They all straighten.)

BETTY. And the doctors have advised against congregating in confined spaces…

(They all move slightly apart.)

HAGGARD. That's just a rumour, Betty.

BETTY. Is it? When I came through the streets tonight I saw a rider astride a pale horse.

RODERICK. A pale horse!

HAGGARD. Why do you blanch, Roderick?

RODERICK. Father, the rider of the pale horse is death.

(The **SEAMAN** *turns towards them.)*

SEAMAN. Don't talk to me of death.

HAGGARD. I wasn't going to.

SEAMAN. I came from Ámsterdam on yesterday's tide. There the pestilence rages and the death carts roll through the streets to the sound of the bell-man and the cries of the afflicted...

(Silence.)

HAGGARD. Well, do you know what I say? I say, be gone dull care. More Madeira, landlord. I know a jest that'll set the table in a roar. What did the Bishop of Durham say to the French whore?

PREACHER. I beg you – respect my cloth.

HAGGARD. *(considers)* No, that wasn't it. I'll whisper...

(He whispers in the **SEAMAN**'*s ear. The* **SEAMAN** *begins to laugh helplessly. Suddenly falls face forward into his food. Silence.)*

HAGGARD. Faith. I've never seen it go better. He's convulsed.

PREACHER. He's not convulsed – he's dead.

HAGGARD. At least he died laughing.

PREACHER. *(examines sailor)* It wasn't your jest that killed him – it was the plague.

ALL. The plague!

(They all leap up and stumble to the door.)

PREACHER. One moment! We can't leave him here.

HAGGARD. If you think I'm going to touch him...

PREACHER. You already have...

*(***GRUNGE** *and* **RODERICK** *move away from* **HAGGARD.***)*

HAGGARD. How do you know it's the plague – have you seen those kitchens?

GRUNGE. Where are the blemishes?

PREACHER. There are no blemishes because the disease has gone inwards – festering and putrefying and raging like a forest fire until the victim dies often with a jest on his lips and a glass in his hand.

RODERICK. Oh, Lord.

PREACHER. We can't leave the poor wretch here with his head in a plate.

HAGGARD. Indeed not – we have some feeling. Grunge will carry him to his chamber.

GRUNGE. Grunge will not.

HAGGARD. Grunge, the contagion is carried on the breath and he's not breathing.

RODERICK. I've heard you can catch it from the privy seat.

PREACHER. No, it comes from filth and squalor.

HAGGARD. You see – you're probably immune, Grunge.

GRUNGE. No one's immune to the plague.

PREACHER. Then I must seek assistance elsewhere. And summon a doctor.

HAGGARD. He doesn't need a doctor – he's dead.

PREACHER. We need a doctor for the living, brother. For we are all in danger here – and to go abroad would spread contagion amongst our neighbours...

(Exit **PREACHER**.*)*

RODERICK. Let's get out of here!

*(***HAGGARD*** catches his arm.)*

HAGGARD. Don't panic, Roderick.

RODERICK. Why not? I can't think of a better time. I'm not waiting for the boils and the blemishes – and I'm certainly not hanging about for the putrefying and the festering.

HAGGARD. Keep your voice down. If they find out we've been in contact with this man we'll be outcasts. We'll be walled up over Christmas and fed through a grill. No, we must leave unobserved through yonder casement.

(He points to a high window.)

It leads to a flat roof and safety. I've used it many times to avoid the bailiffs. Now, let's hurry before that canting preacher raises the alarm.

RODERICK. But how do we reach it?

HAGGARD. We stand upon Grunge. You go first, I'll follow.

RODERICK. But what of Grunge?

HAGGARD. What of him?

RODERICK. There's no one for Grunge to stand upon.

HAGGARD. No, Grunge will remain.

RODERICK. That means almost certain death.

HAGGARD. *(sighs)* Roderick, it must be obvious to the meanest intelligence that there is no one for Grunge to stand upon.

(GRUNGE begins to look indignant.)

A gentleman may stand on Grunge but Grunge may not stand upon a gentleman. Ergo, he must remain.

RODERICK. It seems a little harsh.

HAGGARD. Grunge understands.

GRUNGE. Grunge doesn't.

HAGGARD. You disobey me?

GRUNGE. No, I've resigned.

HAGGARD. I'll need three month's notice. Now bend over…

GRUNGE. *(grumbling)* You certainly find out who your friends are when there's plague…

(They start to climb on top of each other and end in an undignified heap as the LANDLORD enters from the kitchens.)

(He regards them suspiciously then turns his attention to the sailor.)

LANDLORD. What's he doing with his head in the plate?

HAGGARD. He's drunk.

LANDLORD. Then we'd better get him to his room.

(He lifts the sailor.)

Well, come on – give me a hand...

(They hold the sailor gingerly – almost between finger and thumb. The LANDLORD *pauses.)*

He looks...dead.

HAGGARD. Food poisoning.

(The PREACHER *enters from the yard.)*

PREACHER. It's not food poisoning. He has the plague.

(They all stand back and the sailor slides to the ground.)

I've informed the Watch and summoned a physician.

LANDLORD. I hope you've been circumspect, preacher. I have a living to earn. Let's get him out of sight...

(The PREACHER *and the* LANDLORD *drag the body out.)*

HAGGARD. Now's the time to panic...

(They make for the outer door. As they open it they see a red cross painted on the door. Several pikes thrust them back into the room and the door is closed.)

Through the kitchens.

*(*BETTY *enters.)*

BETTY. There's no way out, sir. The streets are full of people – they've lit a great fire and no one sleeps.

HAGGARD. Ah, do they fear for my life?

BETTY. I don't think so, sir – they're roasting a pig.

HAGGARD. Unfeeling swine. We're on our own, Roderick. Nothing empties a tavern faster than the plague.

GRUNGE. Unless it's the Black Death.

RODERICK. Or the Raging Pestilence.

HAGGARD. That can get the feet moving...

RODERICK. I don't mind facing death sword in hand but sitting here waiting for the symptoms to appear...What are the symptoms?

HAGGARD. Fever, lassitude and the tokens.

BETTY. Then it takes two courses. It can be quick and peaceful or slow and painful...

GRUNGE. The quick and peaceful isn't that quick – and not always peaceful...

(**RODERICK** *is beginning to wilt.*)

BETTY. But the slow and painful is certainly slow and undeniably painful.

GRUNGE. On the other hand you can recover from the slow and painful – you never recover from the quick and peaceful.

BETTY. No, slow and painful's best – if you can get over the boils...

RODERICK. My God!

GRUNGE. I'm not worried. Not with my abracadabra necklace – proof against any misfortune. I took it from my father's neck the day he was struck down by the Bristol stage.

HAGGARD. Superstitious fool – to put your faith in such trickery. All you need is a simple copper bracelet.

(*He brandishes his wrist.*)

Proof against the plague, St Anthony's fire – and the staggers.

RODERICK. Faith, it's not death I fear but this infernal waiting. If this is to be my last night on earth I want to spend it in the arms of a woman.

BETTY. Well, don't look at me...

(*She exits.*)

HAGGARD. Roderick, with your reputation that was always difficult but with the plague it's well nigh impossible...

RODERICK. (*sighs*) I was thinking of my beloved. If I'm to die they'll find Fanny written on my heart.

HAGGARD. I can believe that, Roderick.

GRUNGE. Which Fanny's that?

RODERICK. What do you mean "which one"?. Fanny Foulacre – it's only now, in the face of death, that I realise how much I love her.

(The **PREACHER** *enters and sits at the table.)*

PREACHER. We've been saying a few prayers over our poor brother.

RODERICK. You didn't get too close?

PREACHER. We had to find out who he was and that meant searching his apparel.

(They move further away from the **PREACHER.** *)*

HAGGARD. Was there any money? Only I was thinking of claiming compensation.

PREACHER. Just a few coins – and a simple copper bracelet.

HAGGARD. What!

PREACHER. A sort of talisman. If only he'd put his faith in the Lord. For tonight I saw an angel on the roof holding a flaming sword.

*(***BETTY** *enters with wine.)*

BETTY. And I saw the pale horse of death.

GRUNGE. And last night, in the yard, I saw a fox kill three hens whilst the rooster crowed.

HAGGARD. Don't you start, Grunge.

PREACHER. All this means that we must turn our thoughts to higher things…

RODERICK. *(hopefully)* You mean the window?

PREACHER. I mean we must make peace –

(The **PREACHER** *starts suddenly.)*

I see him at yonder table!

(They all turn and stare.)

HAGGARD. Who?

PREACHER. He wears a black cloak with a cowl – in one hand he holds a scythe with the other he casts a dice…

(They all stare again.)

GRUNGE. Yonder table?

PREACHER. Aye.

GRUNGE. Which end?

HAGGARD. *(hisses)* What do you mean, which end? Can't you see he's foaming mad.

GRUNGE. It's a vision. It's not given to everyone to see it. I think I've spotted him.

PREACHER. It is Death and whoever sees him is marked.

GRUNGE. No, I must have been mistaken.

PREACHER. I fear for my immortal soul for I have sinned.

RODERICK. You, preacher?

PREACHER. Yes, I was profligate in my youth. I gambled and I fornicated. There, I feel better – they say that confession is good for the soul. And what of you, my son? You look pensive.

RODERICK. *(sighs)* I've whored and I've gambled. And I've had knowledge of a maid on the promise of matrimony. And now, when it's too late I realise all I've ever loved is Fanny.

(HAGGARD has turned away, his hand covering his forehead. Gives a deep sigh.)

PREACHER. And what of you, sir? You've grown silent.

HAGGARD. I've been cruel.

PREACHER. How so?

HAGGARD. I've evicted cripples on Christmas Eve. I've ruined tradesmen and cheated at cards. I've beaten my servant Grunge – returning a smile with a blow. As God is my witness I shall never strike him again. Forgive me, Grunge.

GRUNGE. Right gladly, sir.

PREACHER. And what of you, Grunge?

GRUNGE. *(sighs)* I have robbed my master.

HAGGARD. What?

GRUNGE. I've watered his wine and adulterated his food and sold the produce of his garden for profit. And I've called him a mean, poxy knave in the marketplace.

HAGGARD. You rogue!

(HAGGARD seizes GRUNGE by the throat and wrestles him under the table.)

PREACHER. No!

(He separates them.)

We must forgive each other and we must atone.

HAGGARD. Yes, atone, Grunge before I choke the daylights out of you.

PREACHER. No! We must atone to God.

(He crosses and takes an alms box from a hook on the wall.)

I'm the poorest here. All I have is a few guineas. Let it be given to the poor of the parish.

(He puts the money in the box.)

Now I feel at peace.

(Silence.)

Wouldn't you like to feel at peace, brothers?

(More silence.)

We bring nothing into this world – and we can take nothing out.

HAGGARD. Then Grunge isn't going.

GRUNGE. Here's twenty guineas. All I have.

RODERICK. And here's another twenty. I was saving it for the wedding...

(The money goes into the box.)

(Another silence as they regard HAGGARD.)

HAGGARD. I only wish I could but I'm a poor man...

GRUNGE. Are you?

HAGGARD. What do you mean?

GRUNGE. I thought I heard you chink.

HAGGARD. Chink?

(He shakes his coat.)

You think there's something in the lining?

GRUNGE. I think there's a bag of money there…

(He reaches inside **HAGGARD***'s coat and takes out a bag of coins. Weighs it.)*

GRUNGE. Fifty guineas, I should think.

HAGGARD. I wonder how that got there? I'd forgotten all about it.

GRUNGE. Then you won't miss it.

(He pours the coins into the box.)

HAGGARD. I'm ruined.

PREACHER. No, you're saved. Now, let us swear that whoever survives this night will see that this money will go to the poor of the parish.

(All swear except **HAGGARD***. They regard him.)*

HAGGARD. *(belatedly)* I swear.

PREACHER. Now, I must retire, for I feel my time has come…

(He exits.)

HAGGARD. See if there's any food left in the kitchen, Grunge – all this has given me an appetite…

*(***GRUNGE*** exits to kitchens.)*

*(***HAGGARD*** and ***RODERICK*** regard each other over the box. ***HAGGARD*** rattles it.)*

A considerable sum, Roderick.

RODERICK. Yes, Father.

HAGGARD. Most of it ill-gotten. Serve them right if we took the lot…

RODERICK. It's for the poor of the parish, father.

HAGGARD. Roderick, we are the poor of the parish. See if you can find a ladder to reach that window...

(**RODERICK** *exits.*)

(**HAGGARD** *begins to force open the box. The room darkens. There is the rattle of dice.* **HAGGARD** *peers into the gloom. He sees a hooded figure at the end of the table. He is holding a scythe and casting a dice.*)

HAGGARD. *(uneasily)* Father?

DEATH. Greetings, Haggard.

HAGGARD. Doing a little gardening?

DEATH. A little reaping, Haggard. Should we play. I feel gamesome. Roll the dice.

HAGGARD. What are we playing for?

DEATH. Your life, Haggard.

HAGGARD. Oh. Couldn't we have money on it? Make it more interesting.

DEATH. You'll find it interesting enough. Shake the dice.

(**HAGGARD** *rolls the dice.*)

HAGGARD. Five!

(**DEATH** *rolls the dice.*)

A four. I knew I should have money on it. I've won.

DEATH. No, you've lost.

HAGGARD. I threw a five. How could I lose?

DEATH. Because I maketh the rules... Now you must come with me – for I am death.

HAGGARD. No – take the money instead. There must be almost a hundred guineas here...

DEATH. *(hesitates)* A hundred guineas?

HAGGARD. It's a fortune.

DEATH. It's certainly more than you're worth. Perhaps this once…

(**DEATH** *reaches for the money.*)

(**HAGGARD** *catches* **DEATH**'s *sleeve.*)

HAGGARD. One moment. I didn't know Death took cash.

DEATH. No, it's cheques we don't take... Until we meet again, Haggard.

HAGGARD. Hold! Let me see your face.

DEATH. Take care. The man who sees the face of death sees his own fate.

HAGGARD. I must see!

(**HAGGARD** *pulls aside the cowl to reveal the leering, blemished face of the sailor.* **HAGGARD** *falls back in a dead faint. The* **PREACHER** *enters and picks up the money. The two of them exit into the yard. A moment later* **RODERICK** *enters from the kitchens with a ladder. He sees* **HAGGARD** *slumped over the table.*)

RODERICK. Father! My God! The quick and peaceful.

(**HAGGARD** *straightens up.*)

How do you feel?

HAGGARD. Terrible.

RODERICK. It's the slow and painful!

HAGGARD. I diced with Death, Roderick. I played him for my life.

RODERICK. Who won?

HAGGARD. Who won! What does it look like?

RODERICK. Hard to tell in this light.

HAGGARD. Actually, he did win but that's because he cheats. But he took the money instead.

RODERICK. I didn't know Death took money...

HAGGARD. He takes cash – it's cheques he won't take. Don't you believe me.

(**RODERICK** *gently shakes* **HAGGARD**'s *coat and listens.*)

RODERICK. I believe you.

(**GRUNGE** *enters from the hall.*)

GRUNGE. *(excitedly)* A miracle! The sailor has been cured by the preacher! It was the dropsy – there is no plague...

(**GRUNGE** *exits shouting.*)

(*Silence.*)

HAGGARD. Roderick, we've been tricked.

RODERICK. My twenty!

HAGGARD. My fifty!

RODERICK. Never mind, we still have our lives, father. We can stand under God's heaven and breathe the sweet air. For listen, 'tis morning and the birds are singing. We are no longer outcasts – we can go forth and consort with our fellow man...

HAGGARD. You're right, Roderick.

(*The* **LANDLORD** *enters.*)

LANDLORD. Sir Josh is outside and demands satisfaction now there's no danger of infection.

(**HAGGARD** *picks up a handbell from table. He begins to ring it as he staggers to the door.*)

HAGGARD. (*croaks*) Unclean...unclean...

(*Curtain*)

Scene Two – Dishonoured

(Haggard Hall – Christmas day)

*(***HAGGARD*** *is at the table gnawing away at a chicken leg.* **GRUNGE** *is clearing the table.)*

HAGGARD. *(sighs)* What a day. Two foot of snow and nothing to do but eat. I'm bored, Grunge.

GRUNGE. *(grins)* Things will soon liven up...

HAGGARD. What?

(Noises off.)

(He crosses and listens at the hall door.)

*(***RODERICK*** *enters jauntily.)*

Who are those men in the hall, Roderick?

RODERICK. Sir Josh's party.

HAGGARD. What are they doing here?

RODERICK. They've come for the duel.

HAGGARD. Roderick, it's Christmas Day.

RODERICK. The better the day – the better the deed, hey, father? Besides, Sir Josh didn't want to put it off any longer.

HAGGARD. I thought his temper would have cooled by now.

RODERICK. No, he seems keener than ever.

HAGGARD. But it's out of the question – there's two foot of snow!

RODERICK. They said that was a drawback but I suggested the long gallery.

HAGGARD. You did. That was thoughtful of you.

RODERICK. They suggested pistols – swords being hot work for the older man. I agreed.

HAGGARD. And have you thought of the valuable tapestry in the long gallery?

RODERICK. It's motheaten, Father, and besides, Sir Josh is very accurate. But then, so are you, father. You've never lost a duel.

HAGGARD. I've never faced Sir Josh.

GRUNGE. He never misses. He's killed five men in duels – three with pistols – two with swords. And there's one who'll never walk again.

HAGGARD. Perhaps an apology...

RODERICK. He suggested that. He said he'd sent too many men to glory and would accept an apology. I told him my father would never apologise and damned him for an impudent scoundrel.

HAGGARD. I said that! What did he say?

RODERICK. He said you had an unbridled tongue that would cost you your life.

HAGGARD. He could be right. *(hopefully)* But after all..., many duels are fought where no one is hurt. Pistols are fired in the air and grievances forgotten.

GRUNGE. *(with relish)* Not the last one I saw. That was a real duel, swords, pistols, and teeth.

HAGGARD. Teeth?

GRUNGE. And how it spread. All were killed – even the servants – and two men who'd come into the field to dig turnips.

RODERICK. Enough of these dark thoughts, Grunge. What's for dinner tonight?

GRUNGE. Two cods in oyster sauce – a fowl boiled – a chine of mutton – codling tart and cream.

RODERICK. Sounds tasty. Better bring it forward – we don't want Father to miss it.

GRUNGE. Is that wise, sir? Once he's eaten that he'll make a bigger target than ever.

HAGGARD. I'm not that hungry.

RODERICK. Sir Josh won't find him an easy mark at ten paces, especially if he stands sideways...

*(**GRUNGE** studies **HAGGARD**'s girth.)*

GRUNGE. If he stands sideways he'll be a bigger target than ever. And there's something else you haven't considered...

HAGGARD. What's that?

GRUNGE. If you stand sideways, where's there's two of anything...the ball will go through both. Lungs... kidneys... *(pause)* ...unmentionables.

HAGGARD. Unmentionables?

RODERICK. Don't worry, Father – not all shots are lethal. There are only three fatal areas. The head – the heart and the lungs...

GRUNGE. And the tripes.

RODERICK. Possibly the tripes.

GRUNGE. And the liver.

RODERICK. There is the liver...

GRUNGE. And the lights.

RODERICK. That's enough, Grunge! He may miss you altogether, father.

HAGGARD. He'll miss me all right – because I won't be here.

*(**HAGGARD** begins to slip on a top coat.)*

*(**RODERICK** and **GRUNGE** exchange glances of disgust.)*

RODERICK. You're not going to run, Father.

HAGGARD. Have you a better idea?

GRUNGE. You run now, sir, and you run forever.

HAGGARD. At least I'll be able to run, Grunge. I won't have a bullet in the unmentionables.

(He opens window and looks out.)

I only wish I'd learnt to ski.

RODERICK. And have you thought about me, Father?

HAGGARD. No – at the moment I'm just thinking about myself.

RODERICK. I shall be disgraced. The son of a coward. I shall never be able to hold myself erect again.

HAGGARD. And if I stay, I shall probably be horizontal. He never misses. He's killed five men in duels.

GRUNGE. And one who'll never walk again...

HAGGARD. Will you stop saying that!

RODERICK. And what about Fanny. What will she think of me? She may think that cowards run in the family.

HAGGARD. This one is doing...

(HAGGARD *puts a foot out of the window.* GRUNGE *pulls him back.*)

GRUNGE. You're not looking on the bright side, sir.

HAGGARD. What bright side?

GRUNGE. If you kill Sir Josh your reputation will be made.

RODERICK. And you'll leave the way clear for me to marry Fanny.

HAGGARD. If you think that's such a good idea why don't you kill him?

RODERICK. Because I can't go to Fanny with her father's blood on my hands. She'd never forgive me.

HAGGARD. She won't forgive *me*.

RODERICK. That hardly matters – you won't be here.

HAGGARD. Where will I be?

RODERICK. Abroad.

GRUNGE. Duelling's a hanging offence.

HAGGARD. Perhaps I should go abroad first – save them the trouble.

RODERICK. You can't – there are men with cudgels at the gates. Sir Josh doesn't want any slips-ups...Now I must go and discuss the rules of engagement...

(RODERICK *exits into the hall.*)

GRUNGE. I must say he's very cool.

HAGGARD. It's not his engagement. (*Pause. Studies* GRUNGE) If I were to fall I'll only have one regret – that I haven't left you well provided for, Grunge.

GRUNGE. You haven't?

HAGGARD. I've left so much undone, Grunge. I meant to improve the conditions of the tenants and raise the wages of the servants – yours included, Grunge.

GRUNGE. *(doubtfully)* I didn't know that.

(**HAGGARD** *puts a friendly arm around* **GRUNGE***'s shoulders.*)

HAGGARD. You may laugh at this but I had intended to adopt you...

GRUNGE. Adopt me?

HAGGARD. I was having papers drawn up but now it's all too late... *(sighs)* So much to do...so little time...

(**GRUNGE** *studies him.*)

GRUNGE. You're going to ask me to do something, aren't you?

HAGGARD. A small favour.

GRUNGE. Something unpleasant.

HAGGARD. No...something quite trivial...really.

GRUNGE. What is it?

HAGGARD. When Sir Josh turns to fire – at that exact moment, I want you to shout, 'look out behind you!'

GRUNGE. 'Look out behind you'?

HAGGARD. Yes.

GRUNGE. Won't that distract him?

HAGGARD. That's the intention, Grunge. It's an old trick but it usually works.

GRUNGE. No wonder you've never lost a duel. 'Look out behind you'.

HAGGARD. Perfect.

GRUNGE. But isn't that cheating?

HAGGARD. No... If I shouted it would be cheating but if you shout it I wouldn't be cheating, would I?

GRUNGE. I shout, 'look out behind you' – he turns – and you shoot him in the back? If that's not cheating what is it?

HAGGARD. Gamesmanship. A casual bystander calls out, what can I do about it?

GRUNGE. Nothing – because I won't be calling out. I won't be there. I can't stand the sight of blood – even yours.

(GRUNGE exits.)

HAGGARD. Even mine! The dog!

(RODERICK enters accompanied by SIR JOSH and FANNY.)

RODERICK. Sir Joshua to see you, Father.

HAGGARD. Sir Josh –

(SIR JOSHUA holds up his hand.)

SIR JOSH. Before you vent your spleen on me, sir – allow me to explain. My daughter has pleaded with me to come here – she has persuaded me that there is no necessity for bloodshed. That a written apology will suffice.

HAGGARD. Of course. The ideal solution. Why didn't I think of this before?

RODERICK. We accept. Father, pen and ink for Sir Josh.

HAGGARD. What?

SIR JOSH. No – it's your father who must apologise.

HAGGARD. I'm quite prepared to –

RODERICK. My father apologises to no man. He says what he means and he means what he says. And he damns you for your impudence.

SIR JOSH. Your father goes too far.

HAGGARD. I didn't –

RODERICK. My father doesn't feel he's gone too far – he feels he hasn't gone far enough – and he looks forward to giving you a taste of powder and shot.

SIR JOSH. That is something he may regret.

RODERICK. And so may you. 'He who once did sell the lion's skin was later killed in hunting him'.

SIR JOSH. *(angrily)* What!

HAGGARD. I'm sure we can talk this over –

FANNY. Father, you promised not to be angry.

SIR JOSH. *(sighs)* Very well. After all, this is no more than I expected. You are a proud and haughty rogue, Haggard, but I admire your courage.

HAGGARD. *(modestly)* Thank you.

SIR JOSH. I would not kill you. Your death will only serve to draw attention to this squalid affair. So if your son will agree to forsake Fanny I will call the matter closed.

HAGGARD. *(hopefully)* Roderick?

RODERICK. I can never forsake Fanny. I shall love her to the last day of my life and die with her name on my lips.

FANNY. Oh, Roderick, how brave you are.

SIR JOSH. Then it will mean your father's death.

RODERICK. So be it.

FANNY. Father, you promised there'd be no bloodshed.

SIR JOSH. I'm doing my best, Fanny, but the man is obdurate. *(pause)* There is one other way.

HAGGARD. *(eagerly)* What?

SIR JOSH. If you, Fanny, were to forswear Roderick – never see him again and never mention his name in my presence – I will forgo the duel.

(FANNY moves downstage.)

FANNY. Forswear Roderick?

(HAGGARD nods furiously.)

If only I could. But you may as well ask the moon not to rise and follow the sun – the willow not to lean towards the pool – the flower not to yield its nectar to the bee. I could dissemble but this unruly heart would betray me. I cannot forsake Roderick even if it means his father lying cold in his grave.

(RODERICK takes her hands.)

RODERICK. He'll understand one day, Fanny. He's had his life – he knows that youth must be served. And if his death appeases your father and dispels the clouds that are between our houses he'll feel his sacrifice was worthwhile.

HAGGARD. What!

(**GRUNGE** *enters.*)

GRUNGE. The surgeon's arrived.

(**HAGGARD** *winces.*)

SIR JOSH. Good.

GRUNGE. And a clergyman for the last rites.

SIR JOSH. Splendid.

GRUNGE. And there are two litters for the wounded.

RODERICK. *(loftily)* Then everything's arranged. Well done.

SIR JOSH. Ten paces?

RODERICK. Ten paces will suit us admirably. Is there anything else?

SIR JOSH. Yes, one other thing. You're an impudent young puppy and a thorn in my side and when I've concluded this affair with your father I intend to confront you shortly afterwards.

(*He flicks* **RODERICK** *on the cheek with a glove.*)

You may choose your weapons.

RODERICK. *(aghast)* What?

(**GRUNGE** *begins to titter.*)

(**SIR JOSH** *turns.*)

SIR JOSH. Are you the servant Grunge?

GRUNGE. Yes, sir.

SIR JOSH. My servant extends his compliments and says he doesn't like your face and looks forward to crossing swords with you after the gentlemen have finished.

(*He flicks* **GRUNGE** *with his glove.*)

We await your presence, gentlemen.

(**SIR JOSH** *exits with a protesting* **FANNY**. *The three of them look at each other for a moment and then make a concerted rush for the window. They become stuck in the space. They fall back.*)

HAGGARD. What are we doing? There's a blizzard raging.

RODERICK. I'd sooner face a blizzard than Sir Josh.

HAGGARD. So you're afraid.

RODERICK. Why should I fight him? He's never done me any harm.

HAGGARD. Not yet…

RODERICK. I'm not a man of action.

HAGGARD. Not even for Fanny?

RODERICK. I'm susceptible to pain. I'm only just getting over that blow with the glove.

HAGGARD. And you, Grunge?

GRUNGE. I'm not afraid.

HAGGARD. Aren't you? I thought I noticed you in the general rush to the window.

GRUNGE. It's just that I don't see any point in it.

HAGGARD. The servant insulted you. He said he didn't like your face.

GRUNGE. Well, I'm not that keen on it myself. He's entitled to his opinion.

HAGGARD. You dogs – would you live forever?

BOTH. Yes!

GRUNGE. I'm all for it. I'm hoping for an advance in medical science.

RODERICK. They can cure almost anything these days.

GRUNGE. We could live until we're sixty.

RODERICK. But not with a bullet in the gut. What good would I be to Fanny leaking like a sieve?

HAGGARD. Don't worry, Roderick. I don't want you to fight him. Because if you fight him it means I've lost. And I don't intend to lose. Why is it that the Haggards have never lost a duel?

GRUNGE. Because you cheat.

HAGGARD. Not exactly, well, perhaps a little. But mainly because we use the Haggard Invincible.

(He takes a pistol from the drawer. The pistol has a wide blunderbuss barrel.)

(They stare at it in awe.)

RODERICK. But you've already chosen weapons, father.

HAGGARD. That's the cheating bit... They won't see it coming.

(He hides the pistol inside his coat then takes it out again.)

GRUNGE. What size ball does it take?

HAGGARD. Not a ball, Grunge – nails –

(He begins to load the pistol. He feels the weight of the pistol.)

Beautifully balanced.

(He spins around pointing the pistol. **RODERICK** *and* **GRUNGE** *throw themselves to the ground.)*

*(***SIR JOSH*** *enters.)*

*(***HAGGARD*** *hides the pistol under his coat.)*

SIR JOSH. Ready, Haggard?

HAGGARD. Ready.

SIR JOSH. The pistols are primed and loaded. The seconds have examined them.

HAGGARD. Good.

SIR JOSH. We will be asked to stand back to back, cock our pistols and at a command take ten paces, we will then be asked to turn and fire. Is that agreeable?

HAGGARD. I know the rules.

(They exit.)

*(***RODERICK*** *begins to follow and then turns back.)*

RODERICK. I don't think I can face it.

GRUNGE. It'll soon be over.

RODERICK. But for whom?

GRUNGE. My money's on the squire.

RODERICK. Sir Josh never misses.

GRUNGE. He'll wriggle out of this one. He always does.

(They open the door slightly and listen.)

VOICE OFF. Back to back, gentlemen. Now take ten paces... Then on the count of ten turn and fire. One, two, three, four, five, six, seven, eight, nine...

(There's a violent explosion.)

...ten!

(The voice fades away in an aggrieved groan.)

GRUNGE. What did I tell you?

*(The door opens slowly. **HAGGARD** enters. His face is blackened by gunpowder.)*

HAGGARD. *(hoarsely)* Send for a surgeon!

RODERICK. They have a surgeon.

HAGGARD. No longer – I've shot him.

RODERICK. Is he dead?

HAGGARD. We may need an undertaker – unfortunately I've shot him as well. And one of the seconds...and several bystanders.

GRUNGE. What of Sir Josh?

HAGGARD. Unscathed. Merely blinded by the smoke.

*(**HAGGARD** starts to climb out of the window.)*

See you in Calais...

(Two men with cudgels push him back from the window.)

*(**SIR JOSH** and his servants enter the room armed and angry.)*

*(**HAGGARD** hands his pistol to **RODERICK** who gives it to **GRUNGE** who slips it behind his back.)*

Or possibly not...

(Curtain)

Scene Three – Condemned

(A prison cell – night)

(The flag stones are covered with piles of straw. A barred window overlooks the square. There is a rough table and chairs. A flight of steps leads to the cell door. There are crowd noises from the square.)

(HAGGARD is attempting to peer through the bars. BETTY enters in the company of the jailer CATESBY. She is carrying a small basket and wearing bonnet and cloak.)

(She dabs her eyes.)

BETTY. I've brought you something warming, sir – to get you through until morning.

HAGGARD. *(sighs)* How many times must I tell you? I shall be reprieved by midnight.

CATESBY. *(coarse laugh)* That's what they all say.

(BETTY assembles a bottle and glasses on the table.)

HAGGARD. Any news, Betty? You can't get a paper in this place.

BETTY. George Soper has been poisoned by gypsies after refusing to buy their lucky white heather. And Septimus Brown has been drowned in the Avon while trying to retrieve a farthing.

HAGGARD. I blame the recession. Nothing else?

BETTY. Yes, Squire Haggard is to be hanged tomorrow for duelling and shooting several casual bystanders.

(Noises off.)

HAGGARD. *(listens)* What's the commotion out there?

CATESBY. They're taking their places for the hanging.

HAGGARD. Not mine, I hope.

(CATESBY and BETTY exchange glances.)

BETTY. They've taken all the rooms at The Magpie and Stump – and at The Swan With Two Necks.

CATESBY. It's what I've always said, give the public what they want and they'll turn out.

HAGGARD. Then they'll be disappointed. I have influential friends working on my behalf. I shall be released before dawn – and you can tell that to the hangman.

CATESBY. *(grins)* You already have.

HAGGARD. *(stares)* You're the hangman?

CATESBY. I have to make ends meet – if you'll excuse the expression.

(**BETTY** *supresses a giggle.*)

(**HAGGARD** *frowns.*)

HAGGARD. But what made you choose this grisly career?

CATESBY. I've always wanted to be in showbusiness – and you wouldn't get a better crowd than this at Drury Lane.

(Another roar from the crowd outside.)

HAGGARD. You'd better fetch me another bottle, Betty.

BETTY. Yes, sir.

(**CATESBY** *sees her out of the cell. Another shout from the crowd.*)

CATESBY. They're fighting for places. I knew we should have made it an all-ticket affair. *(pause)* Will you say a few words to them?

HAGGARD. I hadn't thought.

CATESBY. It's usual. But make it short – we don't want to be kept hanging about – we're leaving that to you.

(Suppressed another laugh.)

HAGGARD. You're enjoying this, aren't you?

CATESBY. Just trying to lighten the mood.

(**HAGGARD** *studies him.*)

HAGGARD. Of course – come – have a glass of Madeira.

CATESBY. No, thank you, sir. Not before a hanging. Last time I got so drunk I nearly hanged the parson. Besides, I have to be vigilant – ever since we lost Elusive Edward.

HAGGARD. Elusive Edward?

CATESBY. The only man to escape from this grim place – the only black mark against me.

HAGGARD. I have no need to escape. My friends will save me.

CATESBY. They all say that. *(grimly)* But wait until tomorrow when you ride the three-legged horse foaled by an acorn – when you climb the deadly nevergreen that bears fruit all the year round – when you take a leap in the dark from the scragging post and cry cockles…

HAGGARD. *(gulps)* Cockles?

(A knock on the door.)

CATESBY. Who goes there?

*(**GRUNGE** enters carrying a large hamper. He looks smarter than usual – even a little foppish.)*

GRUNGE. Grunge – to see my master.

HAGGARD. What is it, Grunge?

GRUNGE. I've brought you a boiled leg of ham, a small roasting pig, gooseberry tart, and a bottle of claret.

(He lays the food on the bench.)

CATESBY. Strike me – if he's going to eat all that we'll need a stronger rope. Still, if that's what he wants…after all, he's only getting an artichoke for breakfast. 'Earty choke' – get it?

(The jailer exits laughing.)

HAGGARD. Careful where you leave the food, Grunge – the rats grow ever bolder…

(A hand emerges from the straw and sneaks a pie.)

(They sit on the bench.)

Any news of a pardon, Grunge?

GRUNGE. Not yet.

HAGGARD. Should be through soon.

GRUNGE. They'll be disappointed.

HAGGARD. You mean they want to see me hang?

GRUNGE. They want to see someone hang. Nothing personal. And they have been standing there all night.

HAGGARD. Then they're wasting their time.

GRUNGE. Yes, right. *(hesitates)* But if the worst should come to the worst...

HAGGARD. What do you mean? If the worst should come to the worst...?

GRUNGE. It's the grey mare, sir...

HAGGARD. The grey mare – what of it?

GRUNGE. Well, you'll have no use for it where you're going and she's too slow for Master Roderick and she's just standing there eating up the oats and I wondered if I could have her.

HAGGARD. *(stares)* You, Grunge?

GRUNGE. Yes, and then there's that old carriage standing in the stables. If I were to put them together I could run some sort of haulage business...after you've gone.

HAGGARD. *(aghast)* After I've gone! Grunge, tomorrow I'm to ride the three-legged horse foaled by an acorn – climb the deadly nevergreen that bears fruit all the year round – take a leap in the dark from the scragging post and cry cockles. And you talk about haulage! Have you no feelings?

GRUNGE. Of course I have – I haven't changed.

HAGGARD. *(stares)* No, there's something about you...what is it?

GRUNGE. I don't know what you mean.

HAGGARD. You look different.

GRUNGE. Do I?

HAGGARD. More genteel...more fashionable...

GRUNGE. Well, I have been letting myself go recently...

HAGGARD. Damn me! You've been in my wardrobe!

GRUNGE. The clothes were just hanging there...

HAGGARD. You're wearing my second best coat, you dog.

GRUNGE. Just giving it an airing. We don't want it smelling of mothballs.

HAGGARD. That's not the reason. You didn't think I'd have any need of it after tonight.

GRUNGE. That's not true. I haven't given up hope. *(lowers voice)* I've brought you this...

(He produces a steel tube from his pocket.)

HAGGARD. What is it?

GRUNGE. It may be the means of your deliverance.

HAGGARD. What do you do with it?

GRUNGE. You swallow it.

HAGGARD. What?

GRUNGE. It's an old trick. It lodges in the throat and stops it contracting – then later you're revived by the doctors and a passage booked to the New World.

HAGGARD. An old trick?

GRUNGE. Yes.

HAGGARD. Has it ever worked?

GRUNGE. No.

HAGGARD. And you expect me to swallow this when I can hardly swallow a piece of boiled fish? Thank heavens I need no such device. When my wife throws herself at the feet of the Lord Lieutenant my pardon will be assured.

GRUNGE. She's outside, sir. She's just arrived from Bath.

HAGGARD. Then bring her through, Grunge.

*(**GRUNGE** crosses to the door.)*

I know my wife. She's a born optimist. She'll never give up hope – not while there's a breath in her body...

(**HAGGARD**'s *voice dies away as* **TIBBS**, *his wife, enters, dressed entirely in black. She dabs her nose with a handkerchief.*)

HAGGARD. Tibbs, why are you dressed so? Has there been a death in the family?

TIBBS. Not yet.

HAGGARD. Any news of the pardon?

TIBBS. *(hysterical laugh)* Pardon!

HAGGARD. This does not bode well, Grunge.

TIBBS. There is no pardon, Amos. You're a dead man.

(She totters downstage.)

HAGGARD. Grunge, support your mistress.

(**GRUNGE** *takes* **TIBBS**' *arm.*)

GRUNGE. All is not lost, my lady. Be of good cheer.

TIBBS. How can I be of good cheer, Grunge, when the sun has gone from my life?

GRUNGE. Not yet, my lady – there's still hope.

TIBBS. It is sinking, Grunge. All we have are a few last rays...

(**HAGGARD** *is standing in the background looking appalled.*)

He was a good master to you, was he not, Grunge?

GRUNGE. Indeed he was, my lady, when sober.

TIBBS. He was a man of infinite jest.

GRUNGE. How he'd set the table in a roar.

TIBBS. We shall not see his like again, Grunge.

GRUNGE. No – for tomorrow he stands by the throne...

(**GRUNGE** *catches sight of* **HAGGARD**'s *deepening glare.*)

...if the worst should come to the worst.

(**TIBBS** *leads* **GRUNGE** *further downstage and away from* **HAGGARD**.)

TIBBS. I shall be alone. I shall need a steward, Grunge.

(**GRUNGE** *adjusts his cuffs and smooths back his hair.*)

GRUNGE. I shall be happy to advise you, my lady.

TIBBS. It is a sorry thing when a woman in the full ripeness of her years is left to the bitter winter wind ungarnered.

GRUNGE. Let me make a prophecy, my lady. The sun will shine again and the husbandman will enter the orchard with his ladder and reach for the highest bough where they say the fruit grows sweetest. There will be another harvest, my lady.

TIBBS. Are you sure, Grunge?

GRUNGE. The world keeps turning, ma'am. The birds still build their nests in spring. Young couples still laugh at haymaking. The vixen still seeks out her mate…

(**GRUNGE** *encounters* **HAGGARD**'*s eyes over* **TIBBS**' *shoulder.*)

If the worst should come to the worst…

TIBBS. *(briskly)* Indeed. And if the worst should come to the worst, Amos, I'll be at the window of *The Magpie and Stump.* I shall wave a red handkerchief. That way I shall be with you to the end. Normally I enjoy a hanging but not this one. Now I must go and compose myself.

(*She kisses him lightly on the cheek.*)

Until tomorrow…

(*She almost skips from the room.*)

HAGGARD. I assume from the lightness of her tread, Grunge, that I shall soon be forgotten.

GRUNGE. Not by me, sir. Your memory will always be dear.

HAGGARD. Memory! I've not gone yet! Roderick is going to come through that door at any moment his face wreathed in smiles to announce the King's pardon.

(**RODERICK** *enters frowning. He strikes the table with his riding crop and kicks over a chair.*)

This is not good news, Grunge. What of the pardon, Roderick?

RODERICK. There is none, father.

HAGGARD. What of the gentlemen of the town? Will they not seek a postponement?

RODERICK. I've spoken to the gentlemen of the town. They say a delay would serve no useful purpose.

HAGGARD. It may not serve any useful purpose for them – it certainly wouldn't do me any harm.

RODERICK. They say it would disappoint the mob.

HAGGARD. Oh, excuse me. I wouldn't want to disappoint the mob. I'll come back next week and give an encore. Isn't there enough for them to see at Christmas? Why couldn't they have settled for the pantomime?

RODERICK. One thing is certain. It's time you gave me the gold watch.

HAGGARD. Gold watch?

RODERICK. You always said I should have it. And if the worst should come to –

HAGGARD. Don't you start! Have you no feelings, Roderick?

RODERICK. Of course I have feelings. Have you thought what it'll be like for me? Sir Josh has consented to the match. How will Fanny feel when we walk out of church and find you hanging in chains for all to see? Every time we walk down the High Street there you'll be, swinging in the breeze, a daily reminder of our shame.

GRUNGE. No, Master Roderick. He only hangs in chains for an hour. Then he'll be handed over to the anatomists – and they anatomise him…

HAGGARD. What was that?

RODERICK. No! He'll not be cut up. He'll have a Christian burial, by thunder.

GRUNGE. How so?

RODERICK. I'll get a bunch of sturdy knaves to snatch the body from the hangman.

HAGGARD. Roderick, don't think I'm interfering but wouldn't it be better if the bunch of sturdy knaves snatched my body before they hanged me?

RODERICK. The mob wouldn't permit it – not before – they won't be concerned afterwards.

HAGGARD. Neither will I!

RODERICK. There is one way to cheat the mob…

HAGGARD. Tell me.

(**RODERICK** *produces a bottle.*)

RODERICK. Poison.

GRUNGE. No!

(*He seizes the bottle and hurls it into a corner.*)

That's the coward's way, Master Roderick. I've worked for my master for many years and one thing I know of him – he'll die game…

(*He moves downstage and adopts an eloquent posture.*)

…and with dignity – and his death will be a reproach to those who make our laws and show such little humanity. There'll be tears but there'll be pride too. And we will always remember his going – and perhaps one day, in the fullness of time, there will be reforms through men like him and this squalid public spectacle will be no more.

(**CATESBY** *enters and crosses to* **GRUNGE.**)

CATESBY. I've got you a front seat, Grunge – you won't miss a thing.

HAGGARD. You've got a front seat, you rogue!

GRUNGE. I'd like to be close to you, sir, if the…

HAGGARD. The worst should come to the worst!

CATESBY. I've never seen such a crowd. (*glance at* **HAGGARD**). They say he'll die game.

GRUNGE. He'll die game all right.

RODERICK. My father won't be the first Haggard to take the leap. He'll die game.

CATESBY. He looks a game 'un. Will he address the mob? They like a few last words.

HAGGARD. I'm afraid my muse has deserted me at the moment.

RODERICK. I've prepared a few words, father – if you think they'll do.

HAGGARD. *(dryly)* Thank you, Roderick.

RODERICK. *(stands forward and declaims)* 'Say this of Haggard – that he died like a gentleman and these were his last words. 'I damn all money-lenders, bookmakers and bailiffs with my dying breath and curse all them who brought me down. And this besides, if they want settlement they must follow me to hell, for tonight I sup with the devil.'

(He concludes with a wild ringing laugh.)

(Silence.)

HAGGARD. Yes... I'm not sure if I'll manage the laugh, Roderick.

(CATESBY pats HAGGARD's shoulder.)

CATESBY. He's a game 'un, all right.

(CATESBY exits.)

(HAGGARD looks cautiously towards the door.)

HAGGARD. The time has come to play our last trick.

RODERICK. What last trick, father?

HAGGARD. We must use Grunge's incredible likeness to me.

GRUNGE. *(surprised)* What?

HAGGARD. We could be brothers.

GRUNGE. I didn't know that.

HAGGARD. You must have noticed the likeness, Roderick.

RODERICK. Indeed. Now he's wearing your second best coat – you're almost identical.

HAGGARD. We must use this incredible likeness to our advantage. Grunge dons my wig and hat and I walk out a free man.

RODERICK. A brilliant stratagem, Father.

(They begin to exchange hats and wigs with **GRUNGE.***)*

GRUNGE. What if they hang me instead?

HAGGARD. Then it's a far, far better thing you do now than you've ever done…

*(***RODERICK** *knocks on the cell door.)*

All Catesby will observe is a servant saying a fond farewell to his master.

(The door opens.)

Embrace me, Grunge – not too close. I don't want any of your little friends joining me…

*(***CATESBY** *enters with* **BETTY.***)*

*(***BETTY** *is carrying another bottle of wine.)*

*(***HAGGARD** *crosses, his face buried in a handkerchief and sniffling.)*

BETTY. *(laughs)* Why, sir – why are you wearing Mr Grunge's hat?

*(***CATESBY** *takes* **HAGGARD** *by the shoulder and throws him back into the room.)*

CATESBY. There'll be no more escapes – not on my watch. There's too many visitors… Out you go…

(He pushes **RODERICK** *and* **GRUNGE** *out of the door.)*

RODERICK. Be of good heart, father.

*(***CATESBY** *follows them and slams the door.)*

*(***HAGGARD** *regards* **BETTY.***)*

*(***BETTY** *pours the wine)*

BETTY. Sorry, sir.

HAGGARD. I'm in grave danger, Betty.

BETTY. I know, sir. They say you'll never see another sunrise.

HAGGARD. Yes... Would you do something for a man in such peril?

BETTY. You have a request, sir?

HAGGARD. It's a strange one, Betty. Would you remove your clothes for me?

BETTY. That's not so strange, sir – under the circumstances. Although, if this is to be your last day on earth should you not turn your mind to higher things, not spend it in debauchery and lust? Is this a fit way to prepare for the judgement to come? On the other hand, if this is your dying wish how can I refuse? To sacrifice my chastity would be a sorry thing but if the cause be good –

HAGGARD. Will you shut up? I simply want to exchange clothes.

BETTY. This becomes stranger...

HAGGARD. I wear your clothes and you wear mine, and then...

BETTY. I know the rest.

HAGGARD. I make my escape.

BETTY. Oh.

HAGGARD. You see, I've noticed our incredible likeness.

(BETTY *looks at him and then back at herself.*)

BETTY. You and me?

HAGGARD. We could be brother and sister. After all, my father spread his favours widely. We could be related, Betty. I have your impish face, your little freckles, and we're both easily moved to tears.

BETTY. I hadn't noticed that.

HAGGARD. What do you say, Betty?

BETTY. I can't disrobe, sir – not here.

HAGGARD. All right – just your cloak and bonnet and apron – and you shall have your own pie shop.

(*They exchange clothes.*)

We must hurry before that dog of a jailer returns. Now to crown it all with my new wig and I'm transformed…

(**HAGGARD** *slips on his wig under the bonnet.*)

(**BETTY** *buttons up* **HAGGARD**'s *coat and sits at the table.* **CATESBY** *enters.*)

(*They freeze.*)

CATESBY. You've been here long enough, mistress.

HAGGARD. (*pipes*) Just going…

(**CATESBY** *catches his wrist.*)

CATESBY. Not before I get a kiss, you jade.

(**HAGGARD** *breaks away.*)

HAGGARD. Lips that have touched liquor shall never touch mine.

CATESBY. You never used to be so refined.

HAGGARD. I've changed.

CATESBY. You haven't changed, you minx.

HAGGARD. Want to bet?

CATESBY. Just one kiss.

(*He embraces* **HAGGARD** *who hurls him across the floor.* **CATESBY** *picks himself up shaking his head.*)

CATESBY. You've been working out.

(**GRUNGE** *enters through the open door having witnessed the scene.*)

GRUNGE. (*foppishly*) You lack finesse, my friend.

(*He puts down his basket.*)

The subject should be approached with delicacy and charm. Allow me to salute you, my pretty…

(*He takes* **HAGGARD** *in his arms.*)

(**HAGGARD** *pulls* **GRUNGE**'s *hat over his eyes, turns him round and boots him across the room.* **HAGGARD** *has almost reached the door when he's confronted by* **RODERICK**.)

RODERICK. *(leers)* Hello, my doxy…

(**HAGGARD** *sighs and throws off the bonnet and cloak.*)

RODERICK. Father?

HAGGARD. If this is what a woman has to put up with I'd sooner hang!

(**BETTY** *snatches up her clothes and dashes from the cell.*)

(**CATESBY** *scowls around the room.*)

CATESBY. No more tricks.

(*He slams the door on them.*)

(**HAGGARD** *returns to the table and sighs.*)

HAGGARD. Careful where you put that food, Grunge – the rats are consuming it faster than I can…

(*A hand reaches out from the straw and sneaks a pie.*)

What news, Roderick?

RODERICK. All is not lost, father. The Lord Lieutenant has arrived at the *Swan With Two Necks.*

HAGGARD. *(excitedly)* Has he come with a pardon?

RODERICK. No, he's come to see the hanging but if I were to present him with this petition begging for mercy we may obtain a stay of execution…

(*He produces a scroll.*)

HAGGARD. Yes, that looks most impressive, Roderick.

RODERICK. Would you care to sign it, Father?

HAGGARD. Well, if you think it will carry any weight…

RODERICK. We need all the signatures we can get.

HAGGARD. How many do we have?

RODERICK. Including mine?

HAGGARD. Yes.

RODERICK. One.

HAGGARD. What! *(studies scroll)* Yours is the only signature, Roderick.

RODERICK. You're not very popular, father.

HAGGARD. Why hasn't Grunge signed?

GRUNGE. Because I don't want to be torn to pieces by the mob.

HAGGARD. They wouldn't do that, surely.

GRUNGE. *(darkly)* You're forgetting the counter-petition…

HAGGARD. What counter-petition?

(**RODERICK** *and* **GRUNGE** *exchange uneasy glances.*)

RODERICK. There are those who think the punishment is not severe enough.

HAGGARD. What! You mean they'd hang me twice, the dogs?

GRUNGE. No, they want to hang, draw and quarter you – stick your head on a pole and burn what's left.

HAGGARD. That's barbaric. Who'd sign a petition like that?

RODERICK. Six thousand four hundred and fifty so far.

HAGGARD. Grunge, you may have the grey mare and the carriage.

GRUNGE. Where do I sign?

HAGGARD. We need more signatures.

(*A ragged figure emerges from the straw. He is chewing on a pie.*)

(*They stare at him in astonishment.*)

EDWARD. I don't mind signing.

HAGGARD. Who are you?

EDWARD. Elusive Edward. The will-o'-the-wisp. You must have heard of me. 'Silent and swift with the agility of a cat. As elusive as a fox. 'Doors will open, doors will close but none shall see the man who goes…' That's me.

HAGGARD. What are you doing here?

EDWARD. I keep getting caught. I'm in for lashing and branding. I couldn't face it. I've been hiding in the straw for six weeks. And it's no joke. What about you?

HAGGARD. They're hanging me in the morning.

EDWARD. Hanging. *(sniffs)* Compared with lashing and branding it's a day off.

*(**HAGGARD** studies him.)*

HAGGARD. Have you noticed something, Roderick?

RODERICK. What's that, Father?

HAGGARD. The incredible likeness.

EDWARD. What?

RODERICK. Indeed! You're almost identical.

HAGGARD. We could be twins. Wear my coat and hat for a moment – let me see…

RODERICK. You'll be astonished at the likeness…

EDWARD. At least I'll be warm…

*(They assist him into **HAGGARD**'s hat and coat.)*

HAGGARD. Truly amazing…

*(**HAGGARD** begins to edge to the door. Knocks.)*

*(**CATESBY** enters pushing **HAGGARD** back from the door.)*

CATESBY. Wait a minute. There's something wrong here.

(He peers at them narrowly.)

Yes, I thought so. I've told you before – only two visitors.

EDWARD. *(promptly)* That's all right – I was just going…

CATESBY. Mind you do. I don't want you slipping back in when I've gone…

EDWARD. I won't…

*(**CATESBY** escorts **EDWARD** out.)*

(The door closes.)

HAGGARD. He's gone! And with my best hat and coat. They'll be hanging me in my shirt sleeves!

RODERICK. No. They won't – I'll seek out the Lord Lieutenant and throw myself on his mercy. And if that fails I'll get you another coat…

(**RODERICK** *exits.*)

HAGGARD. *(sighs)* I'm lost, Grunge.

GRUNGE. No, sir – not yet. Hide under the straw.

HAGGARD. Do you think it'll work?

GRUNGE. It worked for Elusive Edward. Hide under the straw then leave later with the visitors...

(**HAGGARD** *crawls under the straw.*)

(**CATESBY** *suddenly reappears.*)

CATESBY. There's something odd going on.

GRUNGE. What do you mean?

CATESBY. Who was that visitor? The one who just left?

GRUNGE. Who do you think it was?

CATESBY. Was it Haggard?

GRUNGE. The same.

CATESBY. That's a relief.

GRUNGE. Why?

CATESBY. They're hanging him.

GRUNGE. What! I thought you were the hangman.

CATESBY. The mob got him first. It's amateur night.

(**CATESBY** *turns to go and then stops.*)

There's still something strange. When I came in here there was a third man…

GRUNGE. A third man. You want to know the identity of the third man?

(*The Harry Lime theme plays over their heads.*)

(*They stare upwards for a moment.*)

CATESBY. I know it already. It's Elusive Edward, isn't it?

GRUNGE. You're too clever for me.

(*He points to the straw.*)

CATESBY. And I thought it was rats.

(He gives the straw a kick. A cry from **HAGGARD**.
CATESBY *pulls out a dishevelled* **HAGGARD** *from the
straw. He's almost unrecognisable.)*

Elusive Edward!

HAGGARD. 'Doors will open, doors will close, but none
shall see the man who goes'.

CATESBY. I thought so. Well, it's the lash and the branding
iron for you.

HAGGARD. What!

*(***CATESBY** *drags him from the cell.)*

*(***GRUNGE***'s concerned look breaks into a smile and then
a grin and finally a supressed titter.)*

*(***RODERICK** *bursts into the room.)*

RODERICK. Great news, Grunge. Father has been reprieved.
The militia have snatched him from the scaffold.

*(***GRUNGE** *wipes his eyes with his handkerchief.)*

Your tears do you credit, Grunge.

GRUNGE. Thank you, sir.

RODERICK. I can't find father. He appears to have become
lost in the crowd. Do you know where he can be...?

*(***GRUNGE** *is busy stuffing his handkerchief in his
mouth.)*

GRUNGE. *(gasping)* Follow the screams...

RODERICK. What!

(A cry from **HAGGARD** *off.)*

*(***RODERICK** *dashes from the cell. Stage left.)*

*(***GRUNGE** *ceases laughing as* **TIBBS** *enters.)*

(She crosses the cell, giving **GRUNGE** *a winsome smile
and drops a red handkerchief. She exits after* **RODERICK**.
Stage left.)

*(***GRUNGE** *picks up the handkerchief and inhales its
fragrance.)*

(He grins and sings to the tune of 'The Red Flag'.)

GRUNGE. 'The working class can kiss my arse I've got the steward's job at larst.'

(Grunge grins and gives a lascivious wink and follows.)

(Curtain)

The End